PARTY PLANNING

FOR CHILDREN AND TEENS ON THE AUTISM SPECTRUM

of related interest

**Helping Children with Autism Spectrum
Conditions through Everyday Transitions**
Small Changes – Big Challenges
John Smith, Jane Donlan and Bob Smith
ISBN 978 1 84905 275 7
eISBN 978 0 85700 572 4

Get out, Explore, and Have Fun!
**How Families of Children with Autism or Asperger Syndrome
Can Get the Most out of Community Activities**
Lisa Jo Rudy
ISBN 978 1 84905 809 4
eISBN 978 0 85700 385 0

Learning About Friendship
**Stories to Support Social Skills Training in Children with
Asperger Syndrome and High Functioning Autism**
K.I. Al-Ghani
Illustrated by Haitham Al-Ghani
ISBN 978 1 84905 145 3
eISBN 978 0 85700 348 5

**Everyday Activities to Help Your Young Child
with Autism Live Life to the Full**
**Simple Exercises to Boost Functional Skills, Sensory
Processing, Coordination and Self-Care**
Debra S. Jacobs and Dion E. Betts
Foreword by Carol A. Just
ISBN 978 1 84905 238 2
eISBN 978 085700 482 6

**Social Communication Cues for Young Children with
Autism Spectrum Disorders and Related Conditions**
**How to Give Great Greetings, Pay Cool
Compliments and Have Fun with Friends**
Tarin Varughese
ISBN 978 1 84905 870 4
eISBN 978 0 85700 506 9

PARTY PLANNING

FOR CHILDREN AND TEENS ON THE AUTISM SPECTRUM

How to Avoid Meltdowns and Have Fun!

Kate E. Reynolds

Jessica Kingsley *Publishers*
London and Philadelphia

First published in 2012
by Jessica Kingsley Publishers
116 Pentonville Road
London N1 9JB, UK
and
400 Market Street, Suite 400
Philadelphia, PA 19106, USA

www.jkp.com

Library of Congress Cataloging in Publication Data
A CIP catalog record for this book is available from the Library of Congress

British Library Cataloguing in Publication Data
A CIP catalogue record for this book is available from the British Library

ISBN 978 1 84905 277 1
eISBN 978 0 85700 614 1

Printed and bound in the United States

Written in loving memory of my cousin, Scott McLellan.
Dedicated to my children, Francesca and Jude.

Contents

Acknowledgements

I often quote Tom Lehrer's line, 'sliding down the razor blade of life' – that's what I'm doing, and I wish I'd worn reinforced trousers! I didn't. So this section is to thank those who've thrown in some verbal padding, the odd practical cushion and an occasional rhino's hide to deflect the blade.

My daughter, Francesca, heads the list for being my companion through the 'joys' of her brother's autism – I include his full-body cleaning of local streets (otherwise known as meltdowns), jumping in a river and igniting a small house fire.

Where would I be without my parents? Probably in a far less grammatically correct personal world, so thanks to Sandra and Peter Reynolds. Oh! And thanks for the love and support as well.

As the youngest of five children, I could fill the entire acknowledgements with my siblings alone. Shirley's searing wit lifts me. David's intellect, pranks and love of the daft make life fun – even when it's tough. Graeme's dry humour and ability to answer even the most obscure of general knowledge questions keep me buoyant – and informed! Lesley's listening ear, empathy and forthright opinions make her my confidante – she's also pretty witty.

The late Joyce Watson, my children's grandma, was adoring of my daughter and consistently optimistic about my son – something for which I'll always be grateful.

Thanks to my Uncle Gordon and Auntie Anne McLellan who actively supported my efforts to get published – this may not be a literary masterpiece but I got there in the end.

We all do things in life that we regret and only sometimes have the opportunity to remedy our actions – I thank Anne Fligelstone (née Middleton) for allowing me to do this.

Being a single parent to two children with additional needs and having no local family has been a strain. I particularly want to thank Sharon Butler, my friend and neighbour, for her consistent help, donated furniture – and strength to carry my daughter into the house with me!

Lee Wiltshire has provided my family with technical support – resurrecting numerous computers that died, several phones my son has drowned and accessing a huge document I'd inadvertently 'lost', in the nick of time for a deadline.

My friend, Anne Callahan, has wholeheartedly accepted my son – an attitude that can be scarce.

Angela Gabriel has made me laugh with her anecdotes, which, surely, should be the subject of her own book.

Several professionals have prevented my careering into an abyss:

- Sue Turville, Speech and Language Therapist, who enabled my son to be diagnosed early
- my family doctor, Christine Voss of Rowden Surgery, Chippenham
- Jo Burton, Amanda Sperritt and David Sperritt, who run North Wilts Holiday Club on a shoestring and provide much-needed respite for caregivers
- youth workers who run Young Carers, for their support of my daughter, Francesca
- Jean Groves, who is Jude's caregiver
- my son's social worker, Lisa Moore
- Miranda and the late Bob Sidwick, Donna Blackey, Sam MacInnes, Rachel Crowder, Hannah White and the many dedicated staff at The Manor School in Melksham, Wiltshire.

Rosalie Allen used Son-Rise techniques to enable my son to produce his first approximations of words aged five years. (Son-Rise is a play-based programme that focuses on developing a relationship with the child, primarily by joining with them and experiencing their world. It acknowledges the purpose and meaning of repetitive behaviours.) She also peer reviewed this book – thank you.

Vicki Hocquard reviewed my sample chapter and Vicki Wells, who tirelessly fundraises for children with autism at my son's school, peer reviewed my manuscript.

Jacqui Thomas gave me the benefit of her writing experience when it felt like I was trying to squeeze a giant squid into a purse in the final stages of writing the manuscript.

My Bath nursing friends have seen the very worst and the best of me – and they're still around. So thank you to Maggie Ade, Jane Brooke, Sarah Davies, Rachel Howell, Carrie Norton, Vinny Ringrose, Cathy Roberts, Mandy Sharp – and the late Cath Scanlon, whose incisive sense of humour will stay in my memory.

In the words of radio phone-in guests, I'll say thanks to 'anyone else who knows me!'

Kate E. Reynolds
December 2011

introduction

The background

I stepped into the world of autism six years ago when my three-year-old son was diagnosed as being 'on the spectrum' – a phrase that meant nothing to me at the time. The 'A' word (autism) was described as 'classic' and the doctor assured me Jude would be in an institution within a year. He might as well have told me it was a terminal condition, the impact was that great.

Support from professionals was minimal, negative or vague, as if no one felt able to commit to giving advice or daring to suggest how or if my son might improve. I was left feeling utterly alone with my only 'friend', in terms of information, being the internet.

Autism support sites, and the helplines of the major charities (such as, in the UK, the National Autistic Society), seem to be a main forum for learning about autism spectrum disorders (ASDs), therapies and how medical and educational services relate to each other (see Chapter 12). One of the most lively and challenging debates for parents/caregivers is parties – events that once brought fun or enjoyment, now dreaded and anxiety-ridden.

This book is designed to answer some of those questions and help parents/caregivers use parties and social gatherings to the benefit of their autistic kids. ASDs affect individuals in different ways – there's no set pattern. The challenges of children with Asperger syndrome are vastly removed from those whose ASD accompanies complex physical issues, for example. Of course, every child has their own personality, so there is no single presentation of ASDs.

One party I attended brought together these different presentations in a way that would have made a situation comedy. One girl's echolalia repeated in my voice 'Do you want a blackcurrant drink?' throughout the meal, while my son ate nothing but spent the entire time dropping tiny Happy Birthday confetti through the hole in his party hat. The introduction of indoor fireworks led to one child's loud belief that this was 'cat poo' while another child started choking melodramatically and complaining bluntly about the smoke. A boy hated the dark – which was necessary to see the fireworks – my son fixated on trying to touch the matches and one girl couldn't bear the sound of the washing machine from the kitchen. The finale was a boy who dissolved into tears when he didn't get a prize in one of the games.

I hope you can keep your sense of humour as you read through my suggestions and advice!

Clinical information

Research suggests that 1 in 100 children in the United Kingdom has an ASD (Baird *et al.* 2006) and 1 in 88 in the United States (Centers for Disease Control and Prevention 2012) so there is a real chance that, at some point in their lives, most people will host a celebration party where one of the guests is on the autism spectrum.

The focus of this book is primarily parents/caregivers of children and teenagers with ASDs. ASDs are also referred to as pervasive developmental disorders (PDDs) according to diagnosis in the US. These are a range of life-long neurological conditions, which can affect all levels of intellectual ability – savants like 'Rain Man' in the 1988 film of that name are rare. Around 70 per cent of those on the autism spectrum have learning disabilities and nearly half have an IQ of less than 50 (American Psychiatric Association 2000). ASDs are characterized by difficulties in the 'triad of impairments' (Wing and Gould 1979) which are:

1. An impairment of social interaction, such as lack of eye contact, reluctance to be appropriately tactile and following their own 'agenda' of activities.

2. An impairment of social communication, such as delay in speech and difficulty interacting with others.

3. An impairment of social imagination, such as prolonged repetitive behaviours believed to stimulate one or more senses. These are also known as 'stimming', an abbreviated term for 'self-stimulation' (Nind and Kellett 2002).

Sensory processing

The human brain receives huge volumes of information, which it has to interpret and use to instruct the body accordingly. Sensory processing is the brain's ability to effectively interpret input or stimuli using a range of senses spread throughout the body. So, for example, if we put our hands onto something dangerously hot, our pain sensors immediately identify pain, transmit this to the brain, which interprets it, and instructs us to remove our hands from the object. This is achieved in seconds, without conscious thought.

The special senses are touch (tactile), hearing (auditory), sight (visual), taste (gustatory) and smell (olfactory). Other key senses govern skeletal co-ordination (using vestibular and proprioceptive senses) and fine motor functions (combining tactile, visual, vestibular and proprioceptive senses.) All these crucial senses (and more) may be impaired in children with ASDs. This directly affects their ability to efficiently receive and process sensory information and can adversely affect their relationship with the social world.

It's important to understand the difficulties ASD kids may have in order to plan a party and minimize challenges for the children – and you!

Stimming

This term is an abbreviation for self-stimulatory behaviours, such as rocking, arm-flapping, spinning, head-banging or echolalia (when phrases or words are repeated, often out of context). The function of stimming is to increase sensory input when sensory processing is damaged – this calms and soothes the person, usually in distressing situations such as those with overwhelming stimuli (like a party!). It can enable people with ASDs to manage difficult environments or emotions such as anger or anxiety.

Stimming is seen in typical behaviours, such as nail-biting or pencil-tapping. It is the choice of stimming behaviours and the quantity of time during which stimming is used, which differentiates autistic from typical stimming.

Autism as a spectrum

Parties and other celebrations, with a host of stimuli – music, party poppers, crowds of guests, party foods – present a range of potential difficulties to these children and teenagers.

As the name says, ASDs form a spectrum of disability. The extent of disability related to ASDs depends on where the child is located on the continuum of the condition at any point in time. These can range from the non-verbal child, who lacks understanding of words and body language and is overwhelmed by sounds and sights of ordinary social situations; to the child who has advanced speech, vast knowledge of incredibly narrow subjects, but is socially inept, non-specifically feels 'different' and does not intuitively know social norms.

One of the challenges when writing about ASDs is to provide information that can help across the range of presenting conditions. There is no clear line between 'higher' and 'lower' functioning kids with ASDs, aside from examining IQ (see below). From a clinical perspective, it is often difficult to assess IQ because a child's expressive language and social communications may be too challenged. Some ASD kids may be fully self-caring – which seems an obvious criterion for being 'higher' functioning – but have severe language delay or inability to engage in the social world due to their profound interest in a special subject – a feature of being 'lower' functioning.

Most children with ASDs will be middle range or may have some factors that are regarded as 'higher' functioning and some 'lower' functioning. However, I have to give some level of guidance, so I have separated Asperger syndrome/higher functioning autism from lower functioning autism, giving specific suggestions about party planning for these groups.

Asperger syndrome and higher functioning autism

Asperger syndrome and higher functioning autism are defined as existing only in people who have average or above average intelligence, at or above an IQ of 65 (National Autistic Society 2011a). In Asperger syndrome, children will achieve developmental milestones, sometimes ahead of their typical counterparts. A diagnosis of Asperger syndrome, as defined by the American Psychiatric Association and the World Health Organization, can only be given if the child has typical development of verbal language and other cognitive skills. In higher functioning autism, speech and/or cognitive functioning are delayed in childhood (American Psychiatric Association 2000; World Health Organization 1993).

Key signs of Asperger syndrome are difficulties with social communications, obsessive and ritualistic behaviours and poor co-ordination skills and sensory difficulties.

Gender differences

All research confirms a greater incidence of ASDs among males than females, averaging 4:1 in autism disorder (Kanner 1943) and Asperger syndrome (Ehlers and Gillberg 1993).

Boys are five times more likely than girls to be on the autism spectrum when we examine all ASDs (also including Rett syndrome, childhood disintegrative disorder and PDD-NOS [pervasive developmental disorder not otherwise specified]; American Psychiatric Association 2000). This is partly because boys are more susceptible to organic damage than girls, whether through hereditary disease, acquired infection or other conditions. ASDs are widely accepted as being organic in cause (Rimland 1964).

Wing's work found a 15:1 ratio of male to female incidence in Asperger or higher functioning autism disorder and a 2:1 ratio in people with autism disorder and learning difficulties (Wing 1981). Part of the explanation for these findings is that males present with more disruptive behavioural problems than females (Ehlers and Gillberg 1993) and girls often are only identified when they have mental health problems (Gould and Ashton Smith 2011). Females also have more honed social and linguistic skills, so are better at disguising their social deficits and copying typical behaviour, meaning they feature in statistics with greater disabilities (Wing 1981).

The ASD community

Parents/caregivers of children and teenagers with an ASD often choose to support each other, through social groupings such as the National Autistic Society in the UK and the Autism Society of America, both of which have local and national groups.

Depending on the specialized educational establishment, parents/caregivers may invite their child's peers to celebrations, just like typical children do. One supportive aspect of this is that autistic behaviours are 'routine' to ASD parents/caregivers who will think nothing of a child acting out, emotional outbursts, stimming or running away. Put the same behaviours in a typical setting and they might be greeted with anything from horror to condemnation.

Other specialist schools may have a catchment of a large geographical area, which diminishes the likelihood of peers attending a party – or serves as an excuse for them not to!

If an ASD child's party and celebration experience starts badly, it may continue to decline to a point where parents/caregivers dread each birthday invitation and vow never to hold a party for their own child.

When children with ASDs mix with typical kids at celebrations, these tend to be particularly challenging. This is often due to lack of education and empathy, emanating from typical parents and children. A common response is that ASD children are perceived as teaching poor behaviours or will impinge on the learning of their typical peers.

Sometimes typical parents are simply scared of autism. I remember a friend who had happily exchanged play dates with my two children, until my son was diagnosed as having autism. One of the last comments she made following his diagnosis was 'This is just a taste of what's to come' when my son became angry as I removed him from a trampoline. I have rarely seen her since then.

Kids with ASDs in non-specialist schooling may not be noticed by other parents until a party takes place – a social event that may expose an ASD child's differences. For some ASD kids, party invitations are so few, that parents/caregivers jump at the opportunity, which increases the stress involved and the likelihood of challenging behaviours.

Reasons for dreading taking your ASD child to a party
Meltdowns
Meltdowns are huge emotional outbursts, which can be extremely prolonged. Parents/caregivers will describe out-of-control behaviours, involving physical and verbal aggression and damage to property and lasting from minutes to over

an hour – only to recur throughout the day, often without warning or obvious trigger. Meltdowns may appear to develop over ordinary situations and events. However, if the child is verbal and able to locate how or why their emotions became overwhelming, it is often clear that several factors combine and what typical people consider 'ordinary' may not be to that child with an ASD. Without an ability to communicate it is hard to predict when meltdowns will happen or how minor or major they will be.

Once a meltdown is in full swing, the joy of any social event will be wiped out. Parents/caregivers who have had this experience feel the full force of social disapproval or pity and an intense feeling that their child ruined another's birthday or celebration. These are powerful reasons for not wanting an encore.

Lack of social etiquette

The very nature of autism means that ASD children tend to feel more comfortable playing or being alone than interacting with their peers. They also often don't have the understanding of social norms, leaving relatives and friends bewildered or annoyed. Party etiquette, such as singing as the birthday cake is brought in, or the host being the one who blows out the candles, may be wasted on an ASD child, whose impulse might be to elbow their way to the cake and get the blowing done before the singing's even finished – this is my son's forte and overwhelming reason for attending any celebration.

Presents and prizes can cause major issues for children with ASDs. It's become common practice for the party girl or boy to open presents at the party itself. This can prove problematic because an ASD child receiving a gift they don't want may openly reject it because they aren't tuned unto the social etiquette of pretending they like something. ASD kids may protest if they give a present they actually want to keep.

As the gift funder, you might start to wonder if the financial and personal costs are really worth it.

Routine

The party may interfere with the ASD child's routine, which is rarely a consideration with typical children, but ASD kids thrive with predictability. They find the unexpected distressing in a deep sense, which can disrupt their functioning for days. The child may be on a special diet, which isn't catered for at the celebration and causes a period of altered behaviours and extreme autistic tendencies in some children.

Lack of parent/caregiver motivation

Kids with ASDs generally prefer to play alongside than interact with other children and have difficulty with the concept of parties – this makes celebrations a challenge to what are often exhausted parents/caregivers. Although they are strongly motivated by the social pressure to ensure their child doesn't 'miss out' these challenges may seem insurmountable or simply not worth the effort.

Typical children who attend the same party may be mean to your child for autistic behaviours, which they don't understand. So as a parent/caregiver your role becomes a 'guard' for your child, which is depressing and stressful.

Parents/care-givers may also suffer the 'fallout' from public celebrations when ASD kids return home. This is the time when they can release stress in a safe environment – and may do so by physically thrashing their limbs about, breaking objects, throwing things and generally causing mayhem until the stress is relieved and they calm down.

Remember that others may refuse an invitation from your ASD child for these reasons.

The purpose of this book

The purpose of the book is to provide strategies for parents/ caregivers that will lessen the anxiety surrounding social celebrations. It acknowledges that what works for typical children may not work for those with ASDs but gives constructive alternatives. Hosting any celebration can be stressful – throw autism into the mix and hosts start to look like they're terrified of multiple stimuli as well!

The solution for some parents/caregivers is to avoid parties – either hosting or attending them. This is a pity because, if managed well, social events give our ASD children an opportunity to develop social skills. Celebrations give ASD kids a dynamic social setting which extends their social experiences and can be generalized to other situations.

The book is directed primarily at parents/caregivers of children on the autism spectrum, but contains useful advice and tips for people who are planning parties where someone else's autistic child may attend. In addition, teachers, teaching or classroom assistants, child-minders, and health care workers may find this book enables them to give a more effective service to ASD kids and advice or support to parents of children with ASDs.

What this book is not

Much as I would like to give unequivocal answers to all possible situations that may arise during celebrations and parties, I can't. This book is an attempt to address the main issues and give guidance about their prevention and management. I hope that parents/caregivers can dip into this book for advice and ways to rethink how to plan and manage parties for children with ASDs.

Outline of the book

In the first chapter I explore challenges our ASD kids experience at conventional parties. In Chapter 2 I examine the pros and cons of home versus public venues and features that enhance or compromise a party with autistic children. In Chapter 3 I suggest visual invitations as a great way of explaining what to expect and reducing uncertainties that cause anxiety. Chapter 4 has examples of party plans that suit our ASD guests. In Chapter 5 I give a strategy for choosing party activities, which draw on the abilities and allows for the disabilities of autistic children. What to do with those picky eaters or those on special diets? Check out Chapter 6 for ideas!

In Chapter 7 I suggest ways that prizes and party favours can be tackled to make it positive for everyone – and cut out those anxieties. Chapter 8 gives helpful suggestions for our younger ASD kids – many of these will be appropriate for chronologically older children too. Chapter 9 outlines the increasing gap in maturity between our ASD kids and typical children, with suggestions. Finally, in Chapter 10, I tackle the thorny issue of parties for teenagers with ASDs, including the added hazards of alcohol use and sexuality.

Despite all efforts, things can go wrong so in Chapter 11 I outline possible scenarios and solutions, to help party hosts have confidence in dealing with difficult situations. Chapter 12 – the party is over and it's time to take stock. I give concluding remarks and suggest possible routes for further support and advice.

Each chapter highlights the prevention and management of potential pitfalls and ends with a list of 'Top tips'. For easy reference, at the very end of each chapter, there is a boxed area, outlining tips for people inviting the occasional ASD child to a celebration party of typical children. As an aside, I should say that my son is now nine – and is not in an institution!

Notes on terminology

Throughout the book, I refer to 'ordinary, mainstream, normal' people as 'typical'. This is an abbreviation of the medical term 'neurotypical' and more commonly used than 'non-spectrum' at present.

I have also used the following phrases interchangeably throughout the text: 'ASD' and 'autism', and 'kids/children with autism' and 'ASD kids/children'.

Difficult Aspects of Conventional Parties

This chapter describes, in practical terms, how children with ASDs may interpret parties, such as birthday celebrations, Bar/Bat Mitzvahs, Bonfire Night and baby showers. Social events that seem a joy to typical children can be challenging to those with ASDs. The key objective of this chapter is to enable you to think through the possible pitfalls of 'conventional' parties and how many of these can be avoided by prior discussion with parents/caregivers and careful planning.

Whose agenda?

Children with ASDs follow what is often referred to as their own agenda, meaning that they are totally self-absorbed, to the exclusion of others, both children and adults. The kid with ASD will play alongside typical children, ignoring social cues to join in their games.

Autistic children tend to be obsessed with specific things, frequently using objects for purposes other than their intended use. My son is fascinated by cutlery and certain straight items, such as pens and pencils. These so-called 'stimming' behaviours can overwhelm social events and are used by kids with ASDs to soothe themselves in uncomfortable or incomprehensible situations.

These obsessive fascinations can be used to mould aspects of your party. For example, we use plastic cutlery during party meals, which don't fascinate my son like metal cutlery does – so all his ASD guests can eat in peace.

If you choose to have your home as the party venue, you must be aware that children may use certain objects at their own home for stimming – and you may find your precious things are dangerous or damaged in an ASD child's hands.

Personal body space

Kids with ASDs are often unaware of the appropriateness of their actions and invade others' personal space without attaching any social meaning to it. This is particularly problematic in parties where typical children mix with children with autism or where the venue is open to typical kids/adults.

Age is also a consideration, in that teenagers may misinterpret invasion of body space as being a sign of sexual attraction. Typical children (especially boys) may take physical proximity as an act of aggression or a challenge.

Verbal and body language

Children with ASDs lack insight into verbal and body language. This can be especially difficult when autistic children are alongside typical children, whose social communication often hinges on unspoken, subtle body language. The older the child becomes, the more complex the use of verbal language among typical kids, who will employ sarcasm and verbal challenges, which other typical children will understand but kids with ASDs will take in a literal sense.

The gap in communication frequently widens as children get older, when typical kids absorb and gain insight into the nuances of unspoken language, while their autistic peers have to formally learn about body language and the complexities of verbal language.

Inability to speak

Up to 50 per cent of kids with ASDs are non-verbal and those who are verbal may have significant difficulties expressing their needs (Yale Child Study Center 2011). This should be covered in your fact-finding mission prior to organizing the party when you can learn who uses PECS, Makaton or visual cues (see Appendix 2).

Avoid games that rely on verbal skills, unless it is a chant that they do together, or you will disadvantage certain kids and increase the chances of boredom and discomfort, which could precede emotional outbursts or other negative behaviours.

An important aspect of planning the party is signage to identify the bathroom within the house or public building so it is clear where the child needs to head. Nothing ruins a party more quickly for all involved than an untimely puddle on the floor! Make no assumptions about age, either – even teenagers may need this signposting.

Many kids with ASDs continue to use nappies or diapers for a number of years beyond that of typical children. Ensure there are facilities for their parents/caregivers or the child and bear this in mind for activities and games.

Lack of social skills

Kids with ASDs don't have many of the social skills they need to play with others. The most obvious difficulties arise over sharing and turn-taking, which are integral to many games. This is particularly difficult when you select a venue that is used by typical kids at the same time as your party is taking place. The general principle behind enabling autistic children is to use visual guidance and reinforcement to facilitate games.

On a simple level, it is helpful if eating and drinking utensils are labelled with the guests' names, to prevent confusion and unnecessary disputes.

Lack of reasoning skills

Many autistic children lack reasoning skills, which can be even more acute in stressful social situations. Avoid having your birthday child open the presents at any point during the party. This may seem ungracious, but that can be overcome with a small thank you note later. ASD children may not fully understand that their gift is not for them to keep but to give away. It is even more galling to watch 'their' present being opened by another child and kept – especially if that socially inept recipient doesn't appear to like the gift and doesn't hide the displeasure.

It is, after all, only social mores that persuade us to open presents at the time of receiving them. You can explain a change to this convention to the parents/caregivers, prior to the party.

Predictability

Children with ASDs need predictability and are helped by countdowns to an activity ending. This is where the importance of committing to a programme of activities, in a particular order and timing, is paramount. It is all in the planning, which can be outlined in invitations. But the key is to stick to the plan – deviating from a plan, especially having given parents and caregivers the information to enable their child to understand the process of the party, could create real problems at the party itself.

Introducing *ad hoc* activities generally is not helpful, because it undermines the timetable your autistic guests expect. Only when things don't go to plan is it useful to have alternative back-up plans.

Kids with ASDs love routine, so remember that a super-late party or one that lasts a long time may be so disruptive that parents/caregivers may have to decide that their child won't attend. In terms of timing an hour and a half may seem short to a typical child, but ideal to one with an ASD.

Familiarity

Children with ASDs like the comfort of familiarity and actively dislike new places. Encourage parents/caregivers to discuss well before the party what particular small toy or object the child wants to take with them as a 'party friend'. Other parents/caregivers could use the same idea for their own child's party. This repetition and familiarity will help children with ASDs manage future parties.

Of course, there may be safety elements to the idea of adopting a 'party friend' to bring – I am thinking of the autistic boy who insisted on bringing his collection of bicycle foot pedals to a soft play area party! Gaining a relationship with parents/caregivers and enlisting their support will minimize the likelihood of unhelpful toys accompanying their child.

It is always worthwhile discussing with the parents/caregivers how children might react to a given venue before you book it. Take a child with an ASD to the beach and he may examine the grains of sand, even try and count them. Take another ASD kid to the zoo and he may ignore every animal, preferring to focus on a path of small stones leading to the gorilla enclosure. I have experienced both scenarios and nothing could persuade either child to participate in the party or even move from their chosen place, even for food.

Providing snapshots of the building and the dining area, for example, will help familiarize the kid with what to expect. Discussions with parents/caregivers might inform you that taking a different path in the zoo – one which doesn't have tiny stones – could enable an ASD child to participate in your party.

Physical dangers

Although parents of children with ASDs may be aware of their own child's propensity to harm themselves, there is no telling what another autistic child is capable of. It is worth asking parents/caregivers for any specific triggers of dangerous behaviours – they may discover new ones at your child's party, but at least you know you have tried to cover this issue.

Conventional parties frequently involve security issues, such as unlocked doors to the outside or adult guests who are unaware that children with ASDs try to 'escape' or may be prompted to do so by something they don't like at the party. Once away from the party, some autistic kids run as fast and as far away as they can, with clear implications for their safety.

Celebration cake candles, pets, electrical equipment, swimming pools and hot tubs all present obvious dangers to children who have less awareness of personal injury than typical children.

Fear of specific things

This can only be gained in discussion with parents/caregivers prior to planning the party. It is relatively easy to avoid a colour, animal or a shape that provokes fear – but only if you are informed it is a problem from the outset. The last thing your party needs is for the yellow-clad entertainer to petrify one of your guests, simply by his costume.

Lighting

Some children with ASDs detest bright lighting or sunlight, others dislike low lighting. For the quiet area, it is usually a good idea to have subtle or no lighting aside from lit-up, water-bubbling lamps or similar. Allow the opportunity for bright lighting, if that is what's needed by a child in the quiet area – even a bright lamp plugged into the electric socket, rather than a central light, will do.

It may be useful for you to have an enclosed children's pop-up tent or den in a corner of a party room, depending on the lay-out.

Bear in mind that at least one in three people with autism will have one epileptic seizure in their lives, frequently more. Strobe lighting, which can provoke seizures in vulnerable children, should be avoided.

Noise

Loud noises can profoundly disturb some kids with autism. Conventional parties involve the use of blow-up balloons, loud music, lots of screaming/clapping during party games and may involve fireworks. You can include this in the invitation, which is effectively the plan for the party, so children with auditory sensitivities are prepared and can remove themselves or be removed to the quiet area, then return when the noisy activity is over. You may choose, of course, to avoid all noise-making activities – particularly if your own autistic child has this sensitivity.

The numbers of people at any party are important. Many kids with ASDs simply cannot tolerate the noise and multiple stimuli created by being surrounded by large numbers of others. Often a group of five guests is plenty. If in doubt, invite fewer children – and even apply this rule in the teen years. It is worthwhile putting the numbers of people invited on your invitation to pre-warn parents/caregivers or guests with ASDs.

Meltdowns

These are overwhelming emotional outbursts which are common features of autism, especially in younger children but also in non-verbal older kids with ASDs. They characterize less verbally able children, who cannot express their needs or wants, but are trying to arrest attention for their needs. Emotional outbursts also occur when kids with ASDs experience distressing stimuli – and there will be plenty of these at a party. Every action has a purpose, so although these behaviours can have a negative impact on everyone around, they demonstrate distress when the child or teen with an ASD does not have the capacity to show you in other, more socially acceptable ways. Many of these negative behaviours can be prevented by parents/caregivers rehearsing verbally and using visual cues to inform their child what to expect at the party.

Aggression

Aggression is a relatively common characteristic of children with ASDs, particularly those whose verbal and other communication skills are severely limited. It is also much more common in teenagers with ASD, whose behaviours are dominated by hormonal fluctuations, especially testosterone in boys, which heightens physical aggression.

Prevention is the key, trying to anticipate possible problems by preparing your autistic guests for what to expect at the party. You can also take measures to minimize the results of aggression – starting by not cutting the celebration cake at the table!

Hyperactivity

Many children with ASDs are hyperactive. It is always wise to include some sort of physically challenging activity early in the party, even if your own ASD child is not keen on aerobically demanding activities. An inflatable castle/bounce house, soft playing area or swimming are all good ways to burn off some of the excess energy certain children may have.

As with the rest of the plan for the party, have visual cues, which you can use to show when it's time for one child to stop and allow another child to use the equipment – and a large, clear timer so that both children are aware of the process of sharing it.

Whose party is it, anyway?

You may be asking yourself this question, having read the range of possible pitfalls. You may even be wondering if it is worth putting so much effort into a birthday party that seems to have to accommodate so many diverse needs.

First, parties are always an effort – it's just that we usually feel there is a direct benefit to ourselves or our child. Remember that by enabling other autistic children, you are indirectly getting something positive back; the event will run more smoothly and be more enjoyable for everyone.

Second, accommodating other kids' autism may encourage other families where autism is an issue to be more enabling towards your ASD child at a future party. Developing social skills is a process and experiencing parties can be a means of your ASD child growing socially.

Top tips

- Communicate with parents/caregivers effectively before the invitations even go out, to discover potential issues. Chapter 4 about party plans contains possible questions to ask which will help you determine a party best moulded to your guests' needs.

- Communicate effectively with the venue owners or hosts to ensure they understand the need for no change in the planned events.

- Familiarize yourself with the venue before the invitations are sent – look for pitfalls.

- Locate an area to be allocated as a 'quiet zone' – and find resources to equip it well in advance of the party.

- Enlist help. If necessary, ask at local schools or colleges offering child care courses and give students opportunities to help and support to learn – maybe suggest them as a pool for future parties. Offer refreshments, employment references and transport.

TIPS FOR INVITING A CHILD WITH ASD TO A CONVENTIONAL PARTY

★ Communicate clearly with parents/caregivers to let them know which activities are likely to happen at your celebration party. Remember that 'surprises' may disturb your ASD guest.

★ Ensure that you have a quiet area for your ASD guest, should the party become overwhelming.

★ Ensure that the ASD child or their parents/caregivers are shown all facilities at the start of the party, such as the location of the bathroom and the quiet area.

★ Ask parents/caregivers if any particular feature might enable the ASD child to manage the party better, such as a small trampoline or other activity to focus on, should the conventional party activities become uncomfortable.

★ If parents/caregivers are not staying throughout the party, liaise carefully with them about the particular needs of that child and any potential difficulties and take emergency contact details.

★ If parents/caregivers are not staying throughout the party, allocate a rota of adults to watch over the ASD child, either closely or at a distance (see later chapters for advice).

★ Ensure any adults who watch over the ASD child are aware of any potential difficulties, such as a child's propensity to 'escape' from events.

★ Remember that stimming (repetitive, ritualistic) behaviours may seem 'odd' but actually soothe the child in unusual or challenging situations. As long as they are not endangering themselves or others, these behaviours can enable the child to adapt to the party and finally engage in it.

★ Ensure your typical (ordinary, mainstream) children are sensitive to the differences in your ASD kids.

CHAPTER 2

Home versus Public Venues

This chapter examines the advantages and disadvantages of locating a celebration party at a family home or in a public venue, such as a sports or leisure facility. Neither can be wholly satisfactory – the unexpected can always happen – but certain aspects may suit different children with ASD better (whether younger, older, higher or lower functioning).

Hosting conventional parties can be stressful – playing host to a party of kids with ASDs can present a gamut of additional stressors, from security issues to special diets. Some features of home-based and public parties make them less or more anxiety-raising and it is this aspect – stress – that often makes the difference as to where you may want to hold your celebration.

The key objective in this chapter is to present the range of possibilities to raise awareness of the pros and cons of where you choose to hold your party, whether it is for mainly ASD kids or only one or two at a conventional party.

General principles

As with all celebration parties involving children, you need emergency contact numbers for every child. It is better to get these in advance, so that they are not forgotten in the excitement and busyness of the day. This is still important with teenagers, who may have as much if not more potential for challenges, as their younger counterparts.

Ask about any underlying medical conditions – epilepsy is commonly associated with ASDs. Also find out if the child has any allergies. You may not need to deal directly with these, but it will be useful information if there is an accident and a child is admitted for emergency care, before the parent/caregiver arrives in hospital.

Always invite parents/caregivers to attend the party or give their advice about their children/teens, if they are not going to stay with them.

Have plenty of adult helpers and volunteers.

Family home as the venue

Home as a routine

Firstly consider how your own ASD child might respond to having his party at home.

1. Will he be able to understand that routines may be different for just that day?

2. Will he be able to return to his usual routine once the party is over?

3. Will he disrupt the party, expecting to follow his routine, such as where and when he eats?

4. Will he be able to share his toys or games, which you may want to use during the party?

5. Will he allow other children or adults into his bedroom to play with his toys or games?

Make no assumptions about what he will or will not do. Visual cues and social stories (see Appendix 2) may support your child's understanding and your experience will inform you.

Damage

All parties run a risk of damage to property, especially when alcohol is involved in the case of teenagers. Such damage is also a clear risk with children and youngsters with ASDs who may have a tantrum or act out when typical kids would not. Entering or leaving new situations can present challenges to some ASD kids, causing them to act out, throwing anything in reach until they calm down and mentally take on what is happening. Party plans will help, but this type of atypical behaviour can result in unforeseen damage in the home to expensive equipment, pieces of furniture and buildings.

Don't feel the need to be polite and leave everything as usual when you have ASD guests – lock away anything of sentimental or monetary value. The chances are, they won't notice. Remember that it's your house – you can make areas 'no go' or 'out of bounds' using signage and locks. You can identify this on invitations.

Flexibility

Being at home offers you the flexibility to use signage broadly, for example, to identify the toilets you want your ASD guests to use – perhaps the downstairs bathroom, rather than one upstairs. The adaptability of being at home also means that you have extra activities (outdoor and indoor) to distract or focus an ASD kid who is struggling to join in the party, or who has challenging behaviour you had not anticipated.

Spend time creating a quiet area for children with ASDs, which you can adapt or add to during the party, if necessary.

All the planning you have done cannot exclude things going wrong on the day. Being at home gives you the flexibility to deal with any issues with no time constraints, no extra charges and no pressure from proprietors or other users of public buildings.

Preparing and cleaning up

Preparing before and cleaning after the party at home can offer you plenty of time, either end – you can prepare the night before and continue clearing up for as long as you want to, after the event. Of course, other responsibilities in the household may make this more stressful for you.

Simple measures can limit the amount of cleaning you have. The bathroom is one area that most of your ASD kids will use. Don't be embarrassed about putting signs on the waste bin or plastic waste bag, instructing that nappies or antiseptic wipes go in there. Leave out ample baby wipes and toilet tissue – these may be used to play with, but may also prevent your bathroom becoming an excremental disaster.

Leave both hard and liquid soaps on the side – some children with ASD will only use one type and anything that encourages clean hands should be welcomed. Keep a small window open, remembering that a large one might facilitate the escape of a child or throwing out objects from the bathroom to the outside world – a favourite trick of my son's.

Security
Some kids with ASDs use 'escaping' as a means of dealing with what they perceive as difficult situations. This may be a bolt for an open door or a more subtle drifting out of a house in an unobtrusive way. Either way, it can create a huge danger if children do leave because their inability to effectively communicate can place them at risk. Kids with ASDs who do not verbalize are at even greater risk and you should not hesitate to contact the police if a child goes missing from your party, even before contacting the parent/caregiver. Such children would be considered vulnerable by the police authorities.

Often the likelihood of a kid escaping depends on the awareness and vigilance of adults. Although you may lock doors and gates to your home, without someone responsible to monitor them or the children, an escape can still happen. If your ASD child does not leave difficult situations, you may not consider this a potential problem – which is where communication with caregivers is essential.

One way of tackling this issue is to allocate a responsible adult to each child, if their own parent/caregiver is not there. Another way is to allocate an exit to a responsible adult, taking it in a rota, for example, to stand at the front door while guests arrive or leave, then lock and carry the door key.

Allocating one person to each child ensures that the child has a known adult to approach if he has a problem, such as forgetting the location of the bathroom or wanting a drink. This idea of a 'key person' may give the child a greater sense of security if their own parent/caregiver is not there and may limit challenging behaviours.

Safety

Birthday cakes for typical children inevitably have candles on top, which have resulted in burnt fingers, hair or eyelashes in my experience alone. My own son cannot bear to see candles without blowing them out – causing numerous problems at parties, especially when I have had little or no warning of the impending celebration cake. With advance warning, I would remove him from the room and distract him with another activity or go to the quiet room.

As the party host, you have to accept that singing the 'Happy Birthday' song and watching your child blow out candles may not be a positive experience for another child with ASD – and would your birthday boy or girl actually notice if there were one or two absent children for this bit of the party? If so, then pre-empt their disappointment and warn them before the party.

Home parties often have family pets present, which can create difficulties. Many children with ASDs do not have the understanding of typical kids, that there are certain behaviours you do not do around animals – and these children may not learn from bad experiences. My son spooked a donkey while we were on holiday; the creature trampled him before I could pull it off and he was lucky not to be seriously injured. Since then, he has tried several times to wander behind horses and donkeys and tap their hind quarters – the very action that provoked the trampling.

Other kids with ASDs may have their own pets that have grown up with the child and are accustomed to the child's unusual or unpredictable actions. However, put an autistic child with a strange dog, for example, and even a usually calm and unaggressive creature could become scared and attack. Either way, animals and children with autism are not a good mix at parties. If you're at home, have a neighbour mind your pet or put it where it won't be disturbed.

A serious danger for children with ASDs is water; unsupervised swimming pools or hot tubs carry a risk of drowning. Additionally, even autistic children in their late teens may not understand the potentially lethal effects of putting plugged-in electrical devices into water – or they may just try it out to see what happens. Always allocate an adult to guard the swimming pool or hot tub at home or ensure doors are locked to indoor swimming pools.

Windows present a danger to children with ASDs, especially those upstairs and large windows. If you can lock your windows, do so. Only leave small windows open, such as bathroom or kitchen windows, to relieve smells. Remember that windows are as viable as doors to an ASD kid who is trying to escape from a difficult situation.

Kitchens offer great potential for accidents with ASD kids whose fascinations – for example, with flames – can lead them into danger. It is safer to prepare food well in advance and avoid having to cook or heat up food with your ASD guests at the party. If you must reheat, do so using a microwave oven which is usually high on a counter and easier to cool down. Put the kitchen as one of your 'out of bounds' zones and lock away potentially dangerous items, particularly sharp knives and electrical devices.

Discuss carefully with the proprietors any equipment you hire for your party. Ensure you are aware of potential dangers of such equipment and whether or not the hire company will provide a member of staff to attend the equipment. Allocate a responsible adult to rotate and ensure safety.

Public venues
Typical children and adults
A common factor in inducing high stress levels in parents/ caregivers of kids with ASDs is situations when their children encounter typical children and adults. Public venues, by their nature, cater for an eclectic mix of the population, many of whom have little knowledge or experience of ASDs. Often, ordinary people will interpret your child's behaviours as being those of a 'naughty' or undisciplined child, rather than a scared or bewildered child who is struggling to understand their surroundings. The pressure on parents/caregivers to have a child who acts according to social mores and expectations can be immense and therefore highly stressful. This may be a pivotal reason for holding a party in a family home.

Some public venues allow you to hire the entire complex or centre, such as a swimming pool or skating rink. This prevents some of these difficulties.

More adventure
As children get older, they may want more adventurous activities that cannot be provided for at home. Proper safety equipment and trained staff in specialist centres can reduce stressors, since the responsibility passes more to the proprietors of the venue. However, you must ensure that documentation related to your party covers responsibilities of the staff and safety issues. Even this, of course, cannot replace the onus on you, to provide plenty of adult helpers to allow for the unexpected.

Staff awareness
Workers at many public venues will have neither skills nor knowledge of ASDs. Without these, the chances of a child

escaping from the party are greatly increased and there may be misunderstandings that will directly affect the party. I remember one celebration party in which staff deflated the bouncy castle/ bounce house when the food was served. This was a routine and logical action for them – but one ASD child perceived the deflating object as it 'dying' and was inconsolable. It didn't help that, when the girl finally had calmed down, my son decided to reinflate the bounce house – which staff then deflated again!

Unexpected changes are more likely at a venue outside the home or when you depend on outside entertainment within the home. My son attended a pool party some years ago, where the floating inflatable was different from the one used at the same ASD boy's party the previous year. His parents had assumed it would be identical. As this was the main focus of activity and an unwanted change for the party boy, the entire event became consumed by his despair. Staff hadn't realized that they needed to discuss the change with the parents, so they could prepare their son, perhaps by using a photograph.

Unaware staff may believe that older ASD kids have similar perceptions to typical children. They may have no concept that a ten-year-old ASD boy might run out of a building and disappear out of sight without responding to instructions to stop or come back. So the summer or hot weather is a time when fire doors may be left open to circulate air – leaving an opportunity for an ASD child to abscond. One way of overcoming security issues may be to allocate an ASD kid to a responsible adult for the duration of the party.

Overcoming lack of understanding of ASDs is a matter of effective communication. Large organizations are ripe for difficulties in communicating information, whether this is among their own staff or between the organization and you. Pinning down written agreements about service provision increases the likelihood of pertinent information being passed to relevant staff. However, as the host, you have responsibility for overseeing the event and reinforcing the issues around ASDs for staff at the venue during the party.

First Aid

Due to corporate obligations, public venues have trained First Aiders on call for all emergencies. Epilepsy is a common feature of ASDs and these staff will be able to administer immediate assistance should a child have a seizure during the party, while waiting for emergency response teams.

Fire regulations

Workers at public venues are fully briefed about what to do if there's a fire. However, the child with ASD may have a different perception of what is happening in this emergency and it is worth informing parent/caregivers of the procedures should a fire occur.

Geography of the public building

By its nature, a public building will have many fire exits and often many entrances, which give opportunity for escape on a grand scale.

Bathrooms may be some distance from your party room or activity, affording another opportunity for escape or for children to get lost. In addition, you may not be allowed to use signage or as extensive signage as you would like, to direct children with ASDs to the toilets. Staff or other users of the venue may also remove signage. Perhaps the easiest solution is to take kids in groups under adult supervision at regular intervals. It is wise to provide ample antibacterial or baby wipes, toilet tissue and soap.

At profit-making public venues, a quiet room or area may only be available at a cost – otherwise, it will be used for another money-making purpose.

Flexibility

A public venue may be unable to provide for specific diets. There may be no resources, should a child be unable to eat the food on offer – and hungry children can be disruptive and act out. Using a venue where you have the option to do self-catering may be a more adaptable choice.

All public venues will give time limits and you may end up paying for extra time or equipment, should things go wrong.

Routine

Either your child or invited guests with ASDs may associate the public venue with a routine. For example, a child may use a sports complex for swimming lessons and be expected to attend a swimming party in the same pool. The ASD may mean that the child finds the change incredibly difficult and acts out accordingly. A way around this is to use invitations as stories, which minimizes the impact.

Children's development

A major advantage of using a public venue for your celebration is that dealing with public events and typical children and adults is almost a rite of passage in the development of kids with ASDs. Overcoming the fear of public situations, with the range of stimuli, the noises, sometimes smells, all associated with public scenarios may help develop an ASD child's ability to cope socially – even if only a slight amount more.

Volunteers

Nothing helps a party run more smoothly like plenty of volunteers. Think about asking a local high school if their upper two years would like to volunteer for experience, free food and an employment reference. You can do a short awareness-raising session about ASDs with them and assure them that they will not be given responsibility for a child, just help out. This can work and could provide a pool of volunteers for other people's parties for ASD kids.

Within the family and friends, ask whoever is willing – the more people on hand, usually the less stressful. Of course, you might want to avoid that relative who only brings stress to any occasion.

Top tips

- Photograph the venue or equipment, for example bounce house or inflatable swim equipment, or key characters, such as a clown.
- Photograph the outside of the building and the toilets.
- Write a social story about what the children will be doing at the party and relate this to the photos.
- Have agreements regarding the venue, such as having a quiet area, put in writing by the venue managers; similarly, make sure you have a written agreement with any company supplying equipment to your home.
- Communicate with parents/caregivers.

TIPS FOR INVITING A CHILD WITH ASD TO A CONVENTIONAL PARTY

★ Invite parents/caregivers to the house or public venue to assess.

★ Photograph the bounce house, inflatable swim equipment or other key equipment.

★ Consider raising awareness among other adults who will be attending the party regarding, for example, hot drinks, expectations of behaviour.

★ Communicate with parents/caregivers.

CHAPTER 3

Using Party invitations as Visual Aids

This chapter will outline how you can use invitations as visual aids that will enable your ASD guests to understand what to expect at your celebration. Higher functioning/Asperger kids may not need detailed drawings; words may be enough for the process of a party but they often appreciate photos of inflatables or venues of parties.

Visual aids

These are visual prompts, such as a series of pictures in sequential order, showing what is going to happen – sometimes called visual timetabling. Kids with ASDs generally are more visually than verbally acute, so pictures are used with written words to enable understanding. The visual abilities of most children with ASD are underpinned by the Picture Exchange Communication System and aspects of Makaton sign language (see Appendix 2).

You can use this visual acuteness and the familiarity that most ASD kids have with visual timetabling in your invitations (see Figure 3.1 for an example).

To _____ (Name)

Jude invites you to his birthday party

On _____ (Date)

At _____ (Place)

From _____ to _____ (Times)

This is what we're going to do!

Greet Jude and give the gift

Activity 1: Bounce house (30 minutes)

Countdown to deflation of bounce house

Activity 2: Coloured parachute games (30 minutes)

Countdown to end of activity

Washing hands

Figure 3.1 Example of an invitation

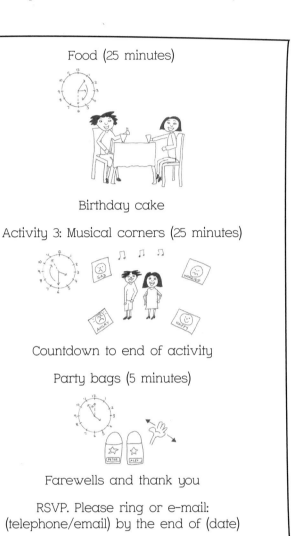

Food (25 minutes)

Birthday cake

Activity 3: Musical corners (25 minutes)

Countdown to end of activity

Party bags (5 minutes)

Farewells and thank you

RSVP. Please ring or e-mail:
(telephone/email) by the end of (date)

Figure 3.1 Example of an invitation (cont.)

Party Plans

The purpose of this chapter is to enable you to produce a workable plan for your party.

Possible questions for parents/ caregivers prior to the party

ASD kids are as individual as any typical child or adult. Their behaviours can depend on where they are on the autism spectrum for different aspects of their development, their age and any other underlying medical conditions. Communicating with their parents or caregivers is essential to your social celebration. Areas which you should ask about are:

1. What are your emergency contact details?

2. What level of communication skills does your child have? Can he verbalize, sign or use PECS?

3. Does your child have a level of physical disability, for example difficulty sitting up, or balancing when walking?

4. Does your child have any medical conditions (e.g. epilepsy)?

5. Does your child 'escape' from difficult situations?

6. What are the triggers for stress in your child? How do you manage these at home?

7 Does your child have any 'problem' behaviours?

8 Is your child on a special diet?

9 What calms your child if he is stressed? This might be quiet music or lying under heavy blankets.

10 What specific sensory issues does your child have? Remember this can be to sounds, touch, smells, lights or other visual stimuli.

11 Does your child need sensory input (maybe physical stimulation such as trampolining)?

12 Does your child have any dangerous behaviours which can be identified and acted on? For example, if the child climbs shelves, or spends time seeking an escape from wherever they are, you can adapt your organization of the party to accommodate these.

Party plan principles
Social stories
Social stories use pictures to make new situations and people more understandable to kids with ASDs. In the context of your party, they can be used to introduce the concept of giving presents (see Figure 4.1 for an example).

When I go to a party, I take a gift.

Sometimes this is a gift I would like to keep.
I give the present.
The person thanks me and keeps the gift.
I may be sad because I like the present.

But I will be OK.
When it is my celebration, I will get
gifts I like and can keep.

Figure 4.1 Example of a social story

Signage

- No go areas: some children are able to go wherever they like at home, with no restrictions, or their parents/caregivers may use locks – either way, they are not used to 'no go areas'. Remember to use a picture to indicate the meaning as well – a 'halt' hand, perhaps, with the wording 'Off limits' or 'Keep Out'. Red is used to indicate danger or 'No' in public buildings, including schools, so use it in your signage.

- Directions: put the signs at a height your ASD guests will see and use arrows plus a picture (of the bathroom, for example). Green usually depicts 'Go' so is useful here.

- OK/Not OK: send home the sign for 'OK' (Figure 4.2) and 'Not OK' (Figure 4.3) with the invitations for use during the celebration.

Figure 4.2 Sign for 'OK'

Figure 4.3 Sign for 'Not OK'

Rules

Send a list of rules and any sanctions, using pictures and words. For example, see Figure 4.4.

Figure 4.4 Example of list of rules and sanctions

Timings

- Allow plenty of time for each activity – cater for disability and extra time that may be needed, whether for comprehension or repetition of a demonstration.

- Use a physical, visual timer – one with grains of sand is usually more understandable than a digital timer. Identify this for guests.

- Don't be tempted to extend an activity because it's going well – your ASD guests will expect to do every game on the invitation and party plan. If you extend one game or activity, you'll lose time on the next.

Numbers

- Outline the numbers of likely guests.

Welcome and receive gift

- Get your birthday child to welcome and thank for each gift, but not open it – put it out of sight.
- Give name tabs/labels for each child, giving their name either on their front or back – omit this for older/higher functioning ASD kids.
- Show each guest the domestics and point out signage, including bathrooms and the quiet room.
- Show a plan on a wall explaining what will happen at the party.
- Show a list of rules and pictures of unwanted behaviours at the party.

Activities

- Do something that won't be affected if guests are late – not too structured, so children can join in.
- Have regular toilet stops and drinks stops.
- Count down to the end of one activity and the start of the next activity, using a visible plan to show what is going to happen.
- Follow rules about when to give prizes and what to give (see Chapter 3).

Food

- Use named cups and named places.
- Have plenty of adult helpers to ensure sharing and to check that guests with dietary requirements get the right food.
- Serve the savoury first, then the puddings.
- Stop to announce the cake and sing – this allows time for kids who are noise sensitive to be removed to the quiet area.

Final activity

- Party bags. Follow the usual rules about what to give (see Chapter 3).

Farewells and thank you

- Get your child to say goodbye and thank you to practise this social skill. Then hand out party bags.

Greeting and receive gift

Activity 1: Dance to a televized game (30 minutes)

Countdown to end of activity

Food

Cake (20 minutes)

Activity 2: Karaoke using televized
words (30 minutes)

Countdown to end of activity

Cake and favours (10 minutes)

Farewells and thank yous

TOTAL TIME: 1.5 hours

Figure 4.5 Example of party plan for ASD teens

Top tips

- Use pictures as well as words to explain the party plan.
- Send it home with the party invitation and ensure parents/caregivers receive the plan and explain it prior to the party.
- Ask specific questions of parents/caregivers.

- Ask parents/caregivers to stay for the duration of the party if you are in any doubt about your ability to manage their child.

- Design the plan and stick to it!

 TIPS FOR INVITING A CHILD WITH ASD TO CONVENTIONAL PARTIES

★ Use pictures as well as words to explain the party plan.

★ If someone will be making a short speech – perhaps for an adult's milestone birthday – put a time for this to ensure the ASD child is aware and knows it is a no-talking time, or is in the quiet room.

★ Send the plan home with the party invitation and ensure parents/caregivers receive the plan and explain it prior to the party.

★ Ensure that parents/caregivers are fully aware that typical children will be attending the party.

★ Ask specific questions of parents/caregivers (see pp.49–50). These will enable you to include their child fully in the party. Ask them!

★ Managing other people's children at social events can be difficult, irrespective of autism. If you are concerned that you may not have the ability to manage an autistic child at your party, ask the parent/caregiver to stay for the duration.

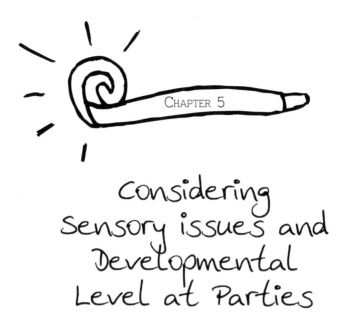

Considering Sensory issues and Developmental Level at Parties

This chapter outlines key challenges in activities and games for ASD children. I offer a strategy for assessing the level and type of activities and games, based on the levels of social communication skills and sensory challenges of your ASD guests. This is demonstrated by a simple table and should use information from parents/caregivers.

Sensory challenges

Sight (visual sense)

Many ASD kids are overwhelmed by visual stimuli, much of which typical children will filter out. Light sense may also be impaired, so children with ASDs may not distinguish between dazzling light and duller lighting – it is all overwhelming.

Some children will scream to obliterate the external noises or fixate their eyes to create a trance-like state that occludes stimuli. Others close off their visual senses by covering their eyes or heads or by squinting.

Sound (auditory sense)

Some ASD kids are extremely sensitive to noise, which they find overwhelming or frightening. This can range from banging drums to constant talking, which prevent the child focusing on tasks or games. Dull background noise to a typical person may be acutely distressing to an ASD child or teen.

Sensory overload may cause severe headaches, anxiety states and meltdowns.

Proprioception

In some children with ASDs, structures such as muscles, tendons, ligaments and joints do not co-ordinate effectively. This dovetailing of efficient co-ordination, which includes spatial and body awareness, is referred to as proprioception and is an aspect of development that can be extended at parties.

In practical terms, this means that children may be unable to sit upright and maintain that position. It can be difficult for a child to sit at the celebration table and problematic for any gross motor activities such as cycling and trampolining.

Other ASD kids may need proprioceptive input in order to keep their bodies calm and their arousal levels regulated, so they will stim to achieve this and need regular physical activity.

Touch (tactile sense)

Commonly, children with ASDs cannot bear certain fabrics on their skin and will continuously wear the same items of clothing for comfort. A friend's child cannot tolerate wearing socks and removes them whenever he is not standing – the material feels like pumice rubbing across his skin because sensory interpretation is distorted. ASD kids who cringe when touched, even lightly, may experience it as scratching or even pain. They may insist on every tag being removed from clothing.

Fine motor skills

Fine motor skills are those needed for intricate actions such as buttoning shirts, when many senses combine, including proprioceptors. Activities that incorporate an element of these senses will help develop them.

In writing, the touch sense combines with a pressure sense – this is the perception of pressure on the body surface. When this processing is damaged, a child may dig their pencil into the paper whenever they try to write or, like my son, do the opposite and hardly make an impression. Holding items can be difficult, either due to lack of hold or squeezing the object. On a practical level, this can result in spilt drinks – so thin plastic party cups or paper party plates can be a problem.

So craft activities, such as gluing or painting, can extend ASD children's fine motor skills, which can be generalized to other areas of life.

Additionally, certain party games can increase use of sensory skills, such as singing or mimicking games. Sometimes sucking hard sweets or using a straw to suck a thick drink can soothe children with ASDs because it gives them oral sensory input, which is soothing. Depending on how supportive the environment, ASD children may feel more encouraged practising these skills at a party than ordinarily.

Development and activities for ASD children

Table 5.1 is designed to enable you to think about the possible activities and games for your ASD child's party, which are given in more detail in subsequent chapters. Your party is likely to be more successful if you plan it around information from parents/caregivers about the level of social communication and physical abilities of your ASD guests. If your party includes mixed abilities, I suggest possibilities in later chapters.

Table 5.1 Development and activities for ASD children

Level of social communication	Activities/Games*
Lower: Little or no verbalization (forming words) Little or no understanding of spoken words Little or no understanding of the social world	Non-competitive activities/games Singing, action songs Moving to music (with or without help) Simple entertainers e.g. puppets Basic crafts (e.g. making shapes in shaving foam) Soft play for special needs
Middle: Short spoken sentences or individual words Understanding the spoken word and instructions Growing understanding of the social world	Simple games (e.g. 'corners', 'tag') Mimicking games (e.g. 'copy me') Highly visual entertainers e.g. clowns Simple crafts (e.g. play dough, blow painting with straws) Non-competitive sports (e.g. trampolining, swimming) Musical games (e.g. 'bumps'), copying dance actions (e.g. 'YMCA'), singing Chasing games (e.g. 'duck, duck, goose', 'four corners', with eyes shut naming the corner that's 'out') Chanting games (e.g. 'What's the time, Mr Wolf?') Turn-taking games (e.g. 'pass the parcel', 'pass the balloon') Sounds games – not too loud (e.g. funny noises)

---

*   See Chapter 8 for descriptions of the rules of most of these games.

	Face painting (check for allergies and sensitivities) Dressing up
Higher: Able to use sentences	Competitive, skilled games Sports with rules Board games
Understands meaning of spoken words	Learn to 'small talk' and initiate conversation (see Chapter 10) Complicated crafts (e.g. building with Lego or clay)
Can follow instructions and rules	Imaginative games (e.g. forfeits, charades) Turn-taking games Skilled musical games (e.g. 'musical statues') Organized sports Dressing up Practising make-up skills (an activity for teenage girls)

The quiet room

All the above games and activities are described in detail in later chapters. The one constant, regardless of age, development, social communication or physical ability, is the need for a quiet room, or at least a quiet area, during any party. This is a crucial part of managing every party because it allows an ASD child to retreat as necessary, reduce anxiety levels and return to try the party experience again. It gives parents/caregivers a place where they can remove their child if they know in advance that a distressing game or activity is about to take place. Quiet rooms do not need every feature below, but these are useful components:

- Low lighting, darkened room with door shut and *no lock inside.*

- Wax lights or lava lamps contain coloured wax in liquid, which forms slowly moving shapes as it heats up. Watching the wax rise and fall can have a soothing effect. Their use should be monitored (because they contain hot fluid).

- Flashing lights, if no known epilepsy, or rope lights. lava lamps and fibre-optic lighting displays are also soothing and give the child a calming object to focus on.

- Bubble tubes in which there is bubbling water with coloured objects floating in it.

- Soft music or CDs of nature sounds.

- Cushions and soft blankets, bean bags or soft mats – anything that can be snuggled into, hugged or hidden under safely.

- Cuddly toys can be used, just like domestic pets that are known to relax people as they stroke them – the same is true of cuddly toys.

- Play tents and tunnels can be filled with cushions and blankets to provide a safe haven for ASD kids, both inside or outside the quiet room.

- Aromatherapy can be therapeutic and useful to calm an anxious child. Lavender is usually suggested as the fragrance is calming. It can be filtered into a room using a diffuser. Although many ASD kids have sensitivities to smells, aromatherapy can reduce these extremes long term or enable them to tolerate smells by drowning them out – for example, a child can carry a plastic bottle of peppermint oil to sniff if smells become overwhelming.

- Watching water flowing can be calming, so any water features that are fully contained are another great addition to your quiet room. You ask for trouble if the water is free to be touched and can be spilled all over your quiet room – trust me, it will be, either during a temper tantrum as the ASD kid enters the room or as a form of excited play once the child has calmed down.

- Any vibrating chairs, mats or other soft furnishings are very popular among our ASD child population and can soothe or fascinate an ASD kid.

Top tips

- Communicate with parents/caregivers to ensure all the ASD kids invited are able to manage planned activities or games – especially if your entire party has one focus.

- Ensure the numbers are manageable, given the levels of support and monitoring ASD kids need.

- Enlist plenty of responsible adults and ensure you are aware of which parents/caregivers will be attending.

- Try to include a physical activity during the party – and time it to be at the beginning of the party when the kids will be most stressed and energetic.

- Remember that age is not always a good guide to which activities are appropriate – it is based on typical development.

TIPS FOR INVITING A CHILD WITH ASD TO A CONVENTIONAL PARTY

★ Communicate to parents/caregivers exactly what main activity you intend having at the party. If it is a sports activity, would the ASD child need good co-ordination and accurate hand–eye co-ordination, which that child may not have and which would therefore put them at a continuous disadvantage?

★ If the activity involves being in a team, ensure the ASD kid is with supportive team players who can actively include the child.

★ Depending on the numbers invited, you may be able to liaise with the parents/caregivers to work out how to educate other guests prior to the party as to the possible limitations of the ASD child. With parents/caregivers' permission, sharing certain information can foster a more supportive environment for the child through education and greater understanding of the issues.

★ Always have a designated quiet room or area, which all guests are aware is for that purpose.

★ Remember that age-appropriate activities for typical children may not be the same as those for kids with ASDs.

Challenging Aspects of Party Food

This chapter describes the purpose of restricted diets that some parents/caregivers feel help reduce symptoms of autism in their children. You may already have adopted a restricted diet as a therapeutic approach for your child's ASD. Catering for other people's ASD kids can be challenging, especially if they are using different diets or food regimes to you.

The key objective is to enable you to create party food that isn't bland and unexciting (unless this is all the ASD child will eat) but which caters for the main restricted diets used as therapy for ASDs.

ASD kids and diet

Sensory issues regarding smell, temperature, taste and texture often mean that children with ASDs dislike certain foods and may resist changes to their diet. In addition, sensory factors affecting their receptors dealing with colours, light and taste cause some ASD kids to eat only bland coloured and flavoured foods or insist on sloppy foods. Some parents/caregivers find that the only way to persuade their ASD kid to eat a particular food is to alter the texture, allowing a previously despised food to be tolerated.

For others, the repertoire of the foods they will eat is extremely limited and very specific. At the age of four, my son had eight food items he would eat, one of which was sausages – but only one brand. He would drink diluted apple juice but nothing else, no matter how thirsty he became – and if it were cloudy apple juice, he would reject it.

Many ASD kids will try to assert particular rules around their eating. A common problem is children not wanting different foods to touch on their plate, which, if allowed, can become entrenched for life.

Parents/caregivers often locate what they believe to be 'trigger' foods which alter their ASD child's behaviour. Commonly these are sugars, caffeine-based drinks such as colas, food colourings and additives.

There are a bewildering array of diets and supplements associated with apparent improvement in symptoms of ASDs, from megavitamin therapy (Adams and Holloway 2004) to omega complex, HNI enzymes and dimethylglycine (DMG) supplements (Kern *et al.* 2001) and various herbal remedies (Golnik and Ireland 2009). Others parents/caregivers report improvements when corn and/or soy are removed completely from the diet. The danger is that in attempting to reduce more extreme autistic behaviours, parents/caregivers can themselves become burnt out with the stress of minutely examining every food item that enters their child's body.

The most common diets adopted, which anecdotally relieve symptoms, are gluten-free and casein-free. It is these that I will address.

Gluten-free and casein-free diets

A body of thought advocates removing all gluten and casein from the diet of children with ASDs. Although rigorous scientific research into the efficacy of this therapy is sparse, there is ample anecdotal evidence of significant improvement in symptoms, such as impulsive behaviours, lack of concentration and verbalization (Whiteley *et al.* 2010). This alone is enough for many parents/caregivers to use restricted diets, usually as part of a repertoire of therapies.

Lack of scientific data is the main reason why conventional medicine rejects elimination diets – without developing a body of scientifically attained knowledge, practitioners tend to avoid a dietary regime that could be mismanaged and cause dietary deficiencies. For gluten-free and casein-free dietary therapy to become embraced by mainstream medicine, it must be proven using randomized, double blind, and clinical trials in statistically significant numbers, to demonstrate a direct comparison between treated and untreated children with ASDs.

The theory

Most dietary regimes are based on the theories that food allergies or deficiency in certain vitamins or minerals cause autistic symptoms. The theory of gluten-free and casein-free diets is that those with ASDs cannot effectively digest these two foodstuffs. Instead, gluten and casein form peptides (chains of amino acids) that can have an opiate effect on the body. This alters neurological functioning, thereby altering behaviours, sensory perceptions and interactions with the world.

Research in the US and Europe has found peptides in the urine of a significant number of children with ASDs (Marchetti *et al.* 1990; Reichelt *et al.* 1981). Urinary peptide tests demonstrate if peptides are being properly digested or not.

New Jersey Medical School's Autism Center found that abnormal immune responses to milk, wheat and soy were more likely in ASD kids than typical children (Jyonouchi 2004). Certainly there is anecdotal evidence that kids with ASDs have fewer episodes of diarrhoea on a gluten-free, casein-free diet (Elder *et al.* 2006).

Although much more thorough scientific research is needed, a study published in 2010 supports the theory that omitting gluten and casein from the diet can have a positive effect on autistic behaviours (Whiteley *et al.* 2010).

What is gluten?

Gluten is a protein found in the seeds of numerous cereal plants, such as wheat, oats, rye and barley. It also is in durum, bulgar, kamut and spelt – and foods containing these. Less obvious sources of gluten are couscous, malt, soy sauce, teriyaki sauce, artificial flavourings and colours and hydrolyzed vegetable proteins.

Gluten is used in the processing of imitation meats eaten by vegetarians – pork, duck, chicken and beef – because it is high in protein. It is used as the stabilizing agent in ice creams and sauces, such as ketchup.

Most bread, flours, biscuits, cakes, doughnuts, croutons and pizza contain gluten – although there are substitutes for gluten in products now.

It is worthwhile noting that gluten is found in play dough as well as some stickers and stamps.

What is casein?

Casein is the primary protein found in milk and milk products such as yoghurts, cheeses, margarines, butters, creams and wheys. It is added to foods which do not appear to be milk products, such as hot dogs and soy cheese in the form of caseinate.

Most parents/caregivers will give calcium supplements if they choose to remove all casein from their ASD child's diet.

How to implement the diet

Those who advocate a gluten-free, casein-free diet suggest removing one of these proteins at a time from the diet. It can take up to six months for the human body to be rid of gluten after the implementation of an exclusion diet, so assessment should take place after this period. However, casein will clear from the body more quickly, so it is generally accepted that it is preferable to remove this milk protein first from the dietary intake.

Some parents/caregivers will remove all gluten and casein at once. The disadvantage of this action is that it is impossible to tell which protein removal caused any improvements in symptoms – one, both or neither. Generally, it is wiser to incorporate as much variety in food types as possible in the diet of growing children, regardless of ASDs. Even when these proteins have been removed, some suggest that many of the eliminated foods should be reintroduced over time.

Advocates of gluten-free, casein-free diets suggest monitoring and documenting changes in behaviours or other symptoms, such as speech, over six months to discover what, if any, improvements have taken place.

What foods can be eaten?

The following foods can be eaten on gluten-free, casein-free diets:

- rice
- potatoes
- amaranth – this is a pseudo grain that contains no gluten
- buckwheat flour
- vegetables
- beans
- tapioca
- fruits
- nuts
- meat
- poultry

- eggs
- fish
- quinoa – this is a grain substitute containing no gluten; it is available in health food shops and some large supermarkets or hypermarkets
- oil
- corn
- sorghum – this is a cereal crop, mainly used for livestock but also for cooking for human consumption; there are several types, one of which is used in syrup.

Cow's milk can be replaced with soy milk, rice milk, almond milk, green bean or peanut milks. There are also readily available non-dairy margarines, creams and cheeses, both soft and hard.

When cooking for your celebration party it is better not to use seasonings or preservatives which research has linked to sensitivities and exacerbation of autistic behaviours (Strickland and McCloskey 2009).

Alternatives to gluten are readily available today, due to the increased knowledge of and diagnosis of coeliac disease, that is pure gluten intolerance that causes inflammation of the walls of the small intestine. In turn this causes mal-absorption of vitamins and minerals which are vital to health (Coeliac UK 2012).

Regular supermarkets stock specialist, gluten-free flours and products, including breads, pizza bases and biscuits.

Baking for special diets may seem onerous but it need be no more taxing than ordinary cooking. I tend to use trial and error, basing most baking on regular recipes. Remember that gluten 'glues' food together, so in its absence, use more eggs or other binding agents.

Basic sponge cake for celebrations

INGREDIENTS

- 200g or 7oz non-dairy margarine
- 200g or 7oz caster sugar
- 200g or 7oz gluten and wheat-free self-raising flour
- 4 medium-sized eggs
- 6 tablespoons of non-dairy milk (e.g. rice or soya milk)
- Half a teaspoon of vanilla essence (check for artificial ingredients)

METHOD

Preheat oven to 200°c, fan oven 180°c or gas mark 6.
Cream together margarine and sugar.
Stir in beaten eggs and vanilla essence.
Add flour and milk.
Bake in greased ovenproof container in oven for approximately 15 minutes.

As you can see from this recipe, for basic party foods it is a matter of replacing commonly used ingredients for non-dairy, gluten and wheat-free substitutes. For more complex recipes there are specialist books and websites.

Safety

One note of caution: barbeques and outdoor cooking of other sorts may be a great idea for typical kids – even an adventure – but it may be wise to avoid them for parties involving ASD kids, especially if their parents/caregivers are not present. My son's fascination with all forms of fire, including candles and lit stoves, is so extreme that he will put himself in danger to be as near as possible. His intention, I think, is to watch and become almost mesmerized by the colours and shapes of the flames – but he has burned his fingertips and singed his eyebrows, despite the fact that I am aware of his acute interest.

Top tips

- Ask directly if any child invited to the party is on a special diet. If your own child is, then create an entire menu based on that – unless another child has an allergy to one of the ingredients.

- ASD support groups (online and in person) have discussions of the pros and cons of certain products on the market and this can be the most helpful way to develop party menus.

TIPS FOR INVITING A CHILD WITH ASD TO A CONVENTIONAL PARTY

★ Ask directly if any child invited to the party is on a special diet. If you cannot adapt the entire menu for one or two ASD guests, most parents/caregivers expect to provide such meals for their kids.

★ Casein- and gluten-free foods are readily available today – check websites for people with coeliac disease (who cannot tolerate gluten) and refer to specialist books, such as Le Breton (2001).

★ In the case of allergies to foods, avoid all likelihood that the allergen will be anywhere in your party menu – an ASD child may be unaware of the implications of the allergy and unable to summon help if affected.

CHAPTER 7

Party Bags, Favours and Prizes

This chapter examines the pros and cons of different gifts and how appropriate they are for autistic kids. While I acknowledge that it is helpful to use all opportunities to enhance the development of our ASD children, I feel that parties are not the time to challenge their stimming fascinations. In fact, I argue that using our ASD kids' obsessions can be useful around gift-giving, party favours and prizes.

Many toys have embedded learning, which can be useful in a world where ASD kids often have functional gifts and activities surrounding them in order to progress their development. Children with ASDs are like typical kids on this – they can enjoy learning without it becoming onerous. As a rule of thumb, check with parents/caregivers – some ASD kids thrive on functional toys, especially in their special interest.

Remember that some ASD kids are wary of surprises, so maybe identify the contents of a wrapped parcel with a picture of what is inside – this includes 'pass the parcel' gifts!

I would always advise to give a prize simply for everyone in an activity or game – this prevents despair and encourages participation.

The key objective is to provide parents/caregivers with suggestions of useful and positive party favours, prizes and gifts for party bags. Children with ASDs have a right to celebrations in the same way as typical children – including party favours and other gifts which form part of the rituals of parties. With a little thought and insight ASD kids can be accommodated and learn to understand this part of social communication in relation to celebrations.

Basic guidance around gifts and ASD kids

ASDs are as individual in their presentation as children themselves. However there are a few common factors:

- Developmental delays can mean that age guides on toys and other gifts may not be relied on for your child with ASD, who will be following their own unique developmental pathway. They may not have the ability to use the 'age appropriate' toy – or may not be interested in it or other toys that most typical children desire at that age. Conversely, if the toy is within their special interest, an ASD kid may be absorbed in a toy that is way beyond their chronological age.

- ASD kids often have little sense of danger.

- Some children with ASDs have 'pica' which means they feel a need to chew and eat any objects, not necessarily foodstuffs – so gifts with small pieces are not a good idea whatever the age of ASD kids with this propensity.

- Equally, some ASD kids like to scatter objects, often rifling through cupboards and drawers to remove their contents – so try to give gifts which don't have tiny parts or which can be disassembled with ease.

- ASD kids commonly have extreme emotional outbursts (meltdowns), so it is helpful to avoid gifts that easily smash.

- Many children with ASDs enjoy ripping paper, either for the sound, the feel or simply to watch it flutter as they throw it in front of their eyes (my son is one of these confetti kids). Typical children are often encouraged to rip open wrapping paper – the difficulty for ASD kids is that many cannot decipher what is acceptable to rip (wrapping paper, scrap paper) and what is not acceptable (books). In lower functioning ASD kids, you may be able to give books with a totally different texture – plastic, solid cardboard or fabric books.

Ideas for prizes and favours

Discover the special interest of the ASD kids at your celebration party and use this to inform any prizes, favours and party bags. Holidays and social occasions tend to be difficult for kids with ASDs because they alter the normal routine of the child's life and have unexpected events – so adhering to their special interest will comfort them in the potentially stressful situation of a party. Party favours or prizes outside their narrow range of interest may actually promote anxiety in the child.

Here are some ideas:

- Try to suspend your own beliefs about what is appropriate as a prize. One ASD child I know delights in the feel of balloons before they are inflated. He likes to rub them against his face and lips. His ideal prize would be a bag of balloons – no matter how unconventional that might appear.

- For the ASD child, there is never enough of their given special interest. Often ASD kids and their parents/ caregivers like to have the same toy item in several rooms in the home. So don't imagine giving yet another of the special interest toys will be a problem.

- Generally, children with ASDs enjoy electronic objects – cheap calculators, for example. However, lower functioning ASD kids may need a direct cause and effect small toy or prize – so push-button electronic talking or noise-making toys, toys that light up by pressing a button, or spinning tops. For higher functioning ASD kids, toys that focus on building, creating and connecting are often a winner.

- As mentioned before, some ASD kids are hypersensitive to sounds. Noisy toys – such as musical toys, hammering or tool toys – can be disastrous for such children.

- Sensory deficits can mean that some children with ASDs cannot tolerate certain textures, whereas others may want to explore feeling objects, so play doughs, squishy balls or other materials would make excellent prizes or favours – there are scented and gluten-free varieties available. Introducing different textures can help de-sensitize ASD kids with sensory issues.

- For children with ASDs who can read, a book is a great idea – especially if it focuses on their special subject. Books offer ASD kids predictability and many enjoy the repetition and rhyming of certain books. Some lower functioning ASD kids will benefit from books with different textures and colours attached, such as foil or fabric. Higher functioning ASD or Asperger kids can be highly literal, so will not enjoy books which involve concepts such as talking or clothed animals, cars or other objects – after all, they cannot do these things in reality. Those higher functioning ASD children or those with Asperger who thrive on detail and facts will be captivated by encyclopedia-type books on their special subject. Books don't need to be expensive – bargain book shops are a good supply – but they should be targeted to be effective.

- Some toys stimulate several senses and can be winners for party bags or favours – small 'slinky' type snakes that can walk the stairs, simple card games, such as 'snap' can help non-verbal ASD kids, but also higher functioning children with ASDs learn to share and take turns. Balls can be fun – but take care what size they are in case they can be chewed or choked on by those who have pica. Shape sorters can enhance visual-spatial skills as well as teach the shapes themselves.

- Small games can fill party bags and directly help ASD kids with social skills. For example, dominoes can encourage turn-taking and joint attention as well as fine motor skills; the same is true of card games. They also teach that losing is an integral part of playing – as well as winning sometimes.

- Many kids with ASDs enjoy predictability, so calendars and puzzles can be a great choice.

- Small and simple puppets can make good favours or prizes that encourage interaction and imaginative play.

- Small musical instruments, such as a drum or pipes, can teach rhythm and melody, which may prove comforting.

- Blocks with raised lettering or numbers can appeal to the need for order in children with ASDs.

- Small toys, such as cars, can also lend themselves to being ordered and sorted according to colour, model, etc. – bringing great joy to the right recipient.

- For ASD kids who like problem-solving, small games that can be used to construct objects are ideal – whether this be a building, an airplane or a bird. Other problem-solving games include 'tic-tac-toe' and 'battleship', both of which include an element of sharing and turn-taking.

- Puzzles and games that have a good chance of captivating ASD kids involve memory games, word finds, mazes and quizzes.

- For children with ASDs who struggle to write, triangular pencil/pen holders or large pens/pencils can enable fine motor skills and fill out a party bag.

- Don't be afraid to use toys for younger children in your party bags. For example, bath toys may be ideal for some lower functioning ASD kids, or those in a child's special subject can fascinate higher functioning children with ASDs.

- Bubbles and their various devices bring great joy to ASD kids – often in those whose age is well above the age of those typical kids who might be interested.

- Many kids with ASDs enjoy balloons, including water balloons. Check with parents/caregivers if they are prepared for the mess of the water variety – and how their child reacts if balloons burst!

- On the subject of balloons, you can create what are referred to as 'squishies' when you fill two balloons, one inside the other, with either sand or flour – again, check with parents/caregivers about the idea of mess before you embark on this party bag treat.

- If you are catering for girls (and maybe boys) paper dolls which you can dress in different outfits can make an ideal party favour, bag-filler or prize.

Perhaps you want to have sweet treats as rewards or prizes. My only word of caution here would be to be aware of special diets (see Chapter 6) or sweets that contain additives. Casein- and gluten-free chocolates are readily available as well as pure fruit sweets – which might prevent your party descending into treat-induced mayhem.

Mistakes in party bags or favours

Don't forget that party bags and favours that you hand out at the end of the party may be opened in the back of a car on the way home, so try to avoid the following mistakes:

- Toys comprised of many small parts, which may be swallowed or choked on by lower functioning ASD kids, or scattered broadly by others with ASDs, adding to the familiar mayhem that often accompanies having a child on the autism spectrum.

- Noisy toys, such as horns and kazoos, for children with ASDs who have sensory deficits in this area. They may also become a focus of stimming behaviours, ensuring their repetition throughout the day.

- Messy toys or games, such as paint sets or bubble kits, are advisable only with parents' permission.

- Games using darts or other devices that shoot – the average child with ASDs does not appreciate the concept of injuring another person in the same way as typical kids.

- Toys whose only purpose is flashing lights, minus the cause and effect of pushing buttons, can become the object of stimming as well.

- Toys that involve flashing lights may be a trigger for epilepsy.

Top tips

- Specifically ask which ASD kids have pica.
- Ask parents/caregivers about underlying medical conditions such as epilepsy.
- Discover from parents/caregivers what their child's fascination is.

- Check if parents/caregivers are prepared for their child to have messy toys or games.
- Give a 'prize' for participating in an activity or game – no matter how small.

 TIPS FOR INVITING A CHILD WITH ASD TO A CONVENTIONAL PARTY

★ Remember that many children with autism have other underlying medical conditions, which include pica and epilepsy. You also to carefully watch epileptic children and summon professional help if necessary.

★ If you can indulge an autistic child's special interest subjects with prizes and in the party bag, you will be half way to giving them a good party experience.

★ Prizes – but not SURprises! It's a good idea to give out prizes even for participating in a game or activity. But surprises can cause anxiety and lead to emotional outbursts – avoid them.

CHAPTER 8

Party Activities for 2–8-Year-Olds

This chapter examines some of the challenges of hosting parties for this age group and what might be appropriate activities. This is a wide chronological age group that is commonly used when addressing play for typical kids – for ASD children there may be even more variation in ability due to slower development emotionally, socially, educationally and physically.

Such kids tend to be highly visual, often hyperactive and needing structure, so the suggestions in this chapter are designed to accommodate these traits.

The main pitfall is distress caused by multiple stimuli – noise, lights and large parties, for example. I suggest you alternate games that require closer physical contact and interaction, which ASD kids find difficult, with gross motor activities that don't involve close proximity and are less focused on interacting socially.

The objective is to equip the reader with ideas for entertaining ASD kids of this age group, while trying to accommodate individual issues for these children.

General features of ASD kids aged 2-8 years

The years from my son's diagnosis at three to about six years of age were some of the most gruelling. In common with many other parents/caregivers of autistic children, I was convinced he had some form of hyperactivity disorder, such as attention deficit hyperactivity disorder (ADHD) as well as being on the autism spectrum.

This is a common experience in the early years when ASD kids seem embattled by sensory stimuli in the everyday world. Whether it is simply maturing or whether once a child has an ASD diagnosis, strategies are put into place to enable social communication and understanding of the world, many parents/caregivers find that the hyperactivity diminishes to some extent as the child gets older.

As a party host, however, you may have to deal with hyperactive behaviours and it is wise to structure any celebrations to incorporate some forms of activities which will harness or guide this trait. Trampolines are a great fallback – they don't need to be large but they do need to be safe. Many ASD kids find the rhythmic motion and predictability of trampolines soothing and it will certainly focus their physical energies. Swings have a similarly comforting effect.

At this early stage in life, ASD kids may 'escape' the stimuli of the social world by:

- hiding – under, behind or in furniture, for example

- covering their heads or bodies – using blankets or coats, for example; often these are heavy materials, which can make the child feel 'grounded'

- removing themselves and soothing themselves by rocking, banging their heads rhythmically, or other 'stimming' repetitive behaviours

- physically removing themselves from the situation by leaving the building

- running away at great speed with no anticipation of or regard for danger – these children are classically called 'runners'
- screaming or shouting out auditory stimuli
- totally losing emotional control – called meltdowns.

These behaviours may continue, even into adulthood. However, older children or adults with ASDs may have better social communication and can be taught ways to deal with stressors or stimuli that are less obvious but still soothing. Even ASD adults who gain insight as to the purpose of the behaviours may still have the impulse to 'stim' – they just learn to control it publicly and use private time to concentrate on stimming.

Temple Grandin, a higher functioning ASD adult, has given tremendous insight into the function of repetitive behaviours. She famously developed a 'squeeze machine' to reduce stress levels in autistics by applying physical pressure to the body, a concept which forms the basis of using weighted clothing on autistic children. Grandin used the device for many hours and was able to demonstrate that a contained therapeutic session prevented a need for constant stimming (Grandin 1996).

ASD kids of this age may be bewildered by parties. Such celebrations may be frightening experiences, full of unpredictable activities and multiple stimuli over which they have no control. This is just at the point when typical children start to understand pleasure derived from parties, the concept of giving and receiving presents and being the focus of attention for their own celebration.

Structuring the party

Many ASD kids, even higher functioning or those with Asperger syndrome, find organizing themselves difficult. They also yearn for predictability and find social contact a challenge. All these factors can be accommodated with small measures.

For example, find out each child's special interest and give them a picture symbol for all items at the party that relate to them. Ensure that the parents/caregivers are aware of these symbols prior to the event and have worked with their child to try and recognize that symbol at the party – this adds predictability to a potentially scary experience. Then use that symbol on their name badge, their plastic cup, their box (see below), their party bag and anything else you want them to know is theirs alone. This prevents social disputes and upset between ASD children who may not be able to articulate if there is a problem over possessions.

Forget the rules for typical children – these can be completely counter-productive. Typical kids may respond to you blowing a whistle for their attention in order to organize the next game – try this at a party full of ASD kids and you could cause mayhem.

Many ASD kids simply don't understand the purpose of games and only derive pleasure from an obscure aspect of them. My son – even at the age of nine years – would prefer throwing a dice around the room to engaging in a board game. For those who do comprehend games, they can teach ASD kids a lot of social skills – if selected carefully and managed well.

If you have one specific activity for the whole celebration, such as swimming or skating, ensure that all ASD kids invited are capable of doing that pursuit. This seems obvious, but I have attended more than one party where an ASD child was simply unable to engage in the main activity. On one such occasion, a girl was terrified of water – she wouldn't even have a bath, it transpired – yet she came to a swimming party and sat for an hour at the edge watching. Even the most meagre splashes of water sent her ducking for cover and clearly stressed her enormously. I remain convinced that this prolonged distress led to her subsequent meltdown when we came to eat the party meal.

Sole activity parties can be extremely helpful if you have a mixed ability group of higher and lower functioning ASD kids. As long as it is not a competitive sport and it is gauged so that the least able child can manage it, an activity can enable a range of disabled children to socially engage.

If you decide to vary the party, choose only two to four activities or games – this allows for having to repeat or demonstrate how a game works or what to do. Always use visual aids and simple wording to explain. For example, have a card that is handed from child to child when it is their turn at the game – this is a physical way of conveying the meaning of taking turns.

In terms of the order of the party, I suggest making the first activity or game a physical one. This enables ASD kids to release some stress that they may feel in an unpredictable situation. It is difficult for ASD children to focus on sitting down and doing mental activities as the very first thing they do in a given event. My son's first school expected the kids in his autism centre to engage in work at a desk the moment they entered the classroom in the morning. My four-year-old became very disruptive and anxious, which affected his whole day in the classroom. On one occasion the routine was altered and the kids did physical exercise in the first session – my son's behaviours were markedly better, which was brought to my attention by staff. The de-stressing effects of physicality are critical to facilitating your party.

Many ASD kids have favourite objects that they like to carry for reassurance in what they perceive as an unpredictable world. Sometimes these special objects are inappropriate to hold when participating in activities. My own child has a fixation with carrying one dessert spoon and two dining forks with him everywhere – they represent a person to him (the spoon is the head; the two forks are the arms and hands). I have tried to substitute these with numerous other objects, including trying plastic cutlery – all of which he has summarily dismissed. Prising them away would cause him extreme distress so I use pictures or visual cues and a fixed place or holder to show where his 'man' will be until he finishes the activity.

If you want to avoid the nightmarish scenario of a child with sharp cutlery leaping up and down on your bounce house or bouncy castle, you can allocate a box for each ASD child to put their shoes or any special things in. Make sure you name the box and, if possible, put a print of the child or a picture that the child will recognize relates to them, on the outside of the box. This does not have to involve great expense – an old cardboard box will do. What it does involve is time and effort – but it will prevent accidents and dramas on the celebration day.

Always have a countdown to the end of any activity – hold up ten fingers and say 'Ten minutes', then announce in the same way when it is eight minutes, etc. This helps ASD kids with transition from one activity to the next – especially if they are particularly enjoying the present activity or game.

It can help to have a 'ritual' at the very end of a game or activity. This may be saying 'goodbye' to the activity, with younger or lower functioning ASD children. It may be a low sound to earmark the ending, for example from a quiet piece of piano music on audio. Using the same piece gives predictability and the low sound level actually entices children to be quieter as they try to listen to the music. Then they are ready to hear about what is going to happen next.

Principles behind the party activities

- Autistic children predominantly are visual in their perceptions, so rely on this strength when communicating information.

- ASD kids tend to need physical challenges to de-stress.
- Lower functioning and higher functioning ASD kids can need very different activities to engage them.
- Use information from parent/caregivers to guide which games or activities to do at the party – you cannot please all ASD kids, but if you have two to four things to do, you maximize the chances that they will engage in some of your party activities.
- Always have a quiet room for de-stressing or for a child who cannot tolerate an activity.
- Structure and commit to paper the order of games, allowing time for children to learn how to play the game or adults to demonstrate the game, however simple. Send a list of games and the order of games to parents/caregivers who may explain the games to their ASD child before the party by means of reassuring the child.
- It is always wise to check with parents/caregivers if any of the proposed games will definitely deeply upset their child – you can then avoid that game or know to remove the child prior to starting the game.

Activities

Organized sports

Many children with ASDs enjoy participating in organized sports. The key is to limit the amount of sensory input, especially physical contact with other children, as would be entailed in football or rugby. Physical contact can feel extremely uncomfortable, even frightening, to ASD kids.

SKILLS DEVELOPED

- proprioception – the effective dovetailing of muscles, tendons, etc. for movement
- turn-taking.

Swimming

This is a popular activity that often transcends more extreme autism. Public facilities frequently provide party sessions with large inflatables or floats for fun. Involve plenty of responsible adults and always follow safety rules around the ratio of adults to children and sufficient lifeguards.

Trampolining

This will almost certainly involve turn-taking due to safety concerns preventing more than one child using a trampoline at any one time. Taking turns can present real difficulties to kids with ASDs, who simply don't understand the social mores around waiting for others to finish before they can experience an activity. They also have difficulty anticipating the future, so can't foresee that they will get the opportunity to have a turn at a later point in time.

If you have enough responsible adults on hand and other activities to occupy the ASD guests until their turn, this may work – but be prepared for challenges.

Bounce houses/bouncy castles

These provide fun without the heartache of turn-taking described above for trampolining.

Soft play centres/play parks

Parties revolving around these activities can be winners. ASD kids often relish physicality, the motion of being on slides or swings or other equipment. The usual problems associated with these play areas are noise and the physical contact that can happen if the area is busy. If the areas are mixed with typical children, unless ASD kids are closely monitored, they can become the butt of jokes or unwittingly upset other children by their lack of adherence to social norms – especially waiting their turn or ignoring rules around personal space.

Themed parties

Themed parties take on meaning for typical kids of this age group. For ASD children, this may be an opportunity for the birthday child or children to indulge deeply in their fascination – be it a movie character or dinosaurs – but other ASD kids may derive no joy from that particular special interest. My son attended a party that was beautifully focused on the subject – pirates – from the 'Ah ha, me hearties' cake to tiny skull and crossbones flags at each table setting. My boy's only concession to the fancy dress theme was a pirate waistcoat – because I sewed it onto his tee shirt. His enjoyment of the party was through holding a series of balloons hard into his face – and attempting to eat every available sausage roll when the children sat down to eat.

Perhaps the best way of approaching the idea of a themed party is to make it a fancy dress party so every child can indulge in their own special interest. Those ASD kids who cannot contemplate dressing up will appear less obvious and those with a special focus can indulge it.

So don't expect a Santa or elf at your Christmas bash and you won't be disappointed – they will turn up at your Easter celebration instead!

SKILL DEVELOPED

- imagination.

Entertainers

Beware the entertainers! You must ensure they are fully in tune with their ASD audience. Suddenly creating loud banging noises, producing flapping birds and doing realistic, scary magic tricks are all likely to halve the audience in minutes – or reduce it to a river of tears.

Working with your entertainers, you can help them perform a highly entertaining show. Balloons shaped into creatures for each of them, a puppet character appearing comically and tricks where things disappear and reappear will be popular – unless these are toys of special interest borrowed from a member of the audience!

SKILLS DEVELOPED

- listening
- observation.

Games as party_fillers

If you're holding a party with several games or activities these are worthwhile party fillers.

Coloured parachutes

These can provide lots of fun as children run under them, are caught under them, hold them up and whoosh them up and down. There is an abundance of games related to parachutes, such as giving one child the role of the 'cat' that must seek out 'mice' while responsible adults hold the edge of the parachute and lift it up and down to hide and unveil the participating children.

SKILLS DEVELOPED

- proprioception
- imagination.

Balloons

These can be incorporated into different games, such as passing the balloons first over the head, then between the legs, from child to child. Passing the balloon person to person holding it only with the knees may involve too much close physical contact and gross motor skills for some ASD kids.

Keeping the balloon up in the air is also great fun for kids with ASDs and requires little physical strength.

Skills developed

- tactile input
- hand–eye co-ordination.

Whacky noises

A bit like forfeits for older or more developed ASD kids, games that involve children copying whacky noises made by the party holder or organizer can be great fun. It is also a social experience that encourages communication through mimicking – which is particularly useful for non-verbal children or those with limited verbal skills.

Skills developed

- verbalization
- listening
- memory.

Giant garden games

The physicality of many ASD kids, difficulties concentrating and dislike of physical closeness means that many ASD children do not enjoy board games. However, if the same game is huge, on a large sheet of plastic, pinned down in your garden or yard, ASD kids can often engage in the activity. This is a very visual way of enabling ASD kids to engage in games.

Games such as snakes and ladders or giant dominoes are available – or you could make one using tarpaulin and copying a small board game.

Skills developed

- proprioception
- sense of balance
- turn-taking.

Messy games

I have read sources who say that messy play is inappropriate for ASD children, whom it is claimed make enough mess without further encouragement at a party. I dispute this – messy games can be fun and a learning experience.

If you're motivated to clear up after children, then try a combination of water and sand or other materials in trays for children to find hidden toys in, or make shapes in with their fingers or just feel the textures. Many ASD kids won't tolerate different tactile experiences, but some will, so this might form part of a range of activities you put on at the party, knowing that it will help increase the ability of an ASD kid to expand their repertoire. Shaving foam, water and cornflour mixed and coloured water or paints can be used.

Another option is more solid materials, such as play dough – easy to make at home in many colours – or other therapeutic putties into which you can wedge shapes or tiny toys for children to find. Make sure you know how many toys or objects there are because an ASD child will want this detail and may continue to search unstoppably without knowing everything has been removed from the putty. Googly eyes can be used to make monsters or creatures from tough putty or play dough or they can be placed in clear therapeutic putty where they will wobble about when the child shakes the putty – this adds to the fun!

Pottery

This doesn't have to involve a rotating wheel and a potter's oven! Children, including those with ASDs, enjoy moulding clay into an object – usually related to their special interest. A note of caution: find highly malleable clay – many ASD kids have fine motor deficits which will be worsened by fighting with tough clay. Also try and get light-coloured clay, so that the children can paint their work of art at home and prevent darker clay altering the colour they want.

SKILLS DEVELOPED

- tactile sensory processing
- visual skills
- understanding of different textures.

Painting

ASD kids can find painting fun. It is not competitive, so is less likely to highlight their sensory and fine motor deficits. You can devise ways of making it more enjoyable and extending the skills of the ASD children – for example, creating a picture using straws to blow liquid paints, sticking and painting dried pasta or different fabrics.

SKILLS DEVELOPED

- oral control
- fine motor skills
- tactile senses
- hand–eye co-ordination.

Water balloons

If your ASD children like water, they'll love these. They can be squashed, thrown in the game of 'catch' or 'hot potato' (in which the balloon is tossed quickly from one child to another, pretending it's a hot potato). When they burst, kids have even more fun – if you're happy to be cleaning up.

SKILLS DEVELOPED

- verbalization – bring this element in by getting the children to call out 'Catch!'
- hand–eye co-ordination increased by catching.

Water games

Water balloons are a fun – if extremely messy – game for parties. This type of activity transcends all levels of autism and can be useful for precisely that. Communicating with parents/caregivers will inform you of any likely difficulties for their ASD kids regarding water balloons. One ASD child in my son's class adores all balloons and uses them for stimming, particularly deflated balloons. Balloons feel soft and pliable, especially against your face, which is where this child gently strokes them. So perhaps water balloons would not be helpful for him. Of course, it is always advisable to tell parents/caregivers of your intentions to possibly cover their children in mess!

SKILLS DEVELOPED

- hand–eye co-ordination
- tactile senses
- social communication, with children joining in a central interest.

Both these and 'catch'/'hot potato' may be challenging to ASD kids if they have auditory sensitivities.

Bubble-making machines

Many children with ASDs adore bubbles to chase, to pop or to blow. This can keep them occupied for long periods and can be combined with chants or words when they, for example, pop a bubble ('Bang, pop, splat') all of which encourage non-verbal kids and give words to less verbal children with ASDs.

Bubbles can soothe many ASD kids, so it's worthwhile having some in store in case of a child acting out or getting distressed, then spending some time in the quiet room, re-emerging to a gentle activity of watching bubbles.

SKILLS DEVELOPED

- verbalization
- hand–eye co-ordination
- proprioception.

Music-based parties

Instruments

Parties involving instruments, singing and music can be highly successful. They can accommodate the range of abilities of ASD kids and can soothe these children. Avoid loud instruments, such as drums or cymbals, which can upset ASD kids with auditory sensory issues. Remember the time when someone bought your child a drum and he banged it continuously for days? That same level of irritation and distress can be caused to ASD kids within minutes. Those ASD kids who cannot tolerate noise can be in a quiet room.

Even basic instruments, such as triangles and tambourines, can give pleasure to children with ASDs. Non-verbal children can find expression in hearing themselves make a sound on a piano or drum. Guided sessions of drumming can be extremely enjoyable and experienced staff can create space for ASD kids to do actions, for example, to the rhythm, or can allow the child to guide the speed of playing according to their actions – all in the context of a party.

SKILLS DEVELOPED

- cause and effect from using instruments
- fine motor skills by holding and hitting an instrument
- hand–eye co-ordination
- verbalization – from singing
- proprioception
- listening/auditory senses.

Singing

For lower functioning or very young ASD kids, singing can give them a way of hearing their own voices without being too exposed or needing to form sentences. My son, for example, was able to sing many words clearly for several years before he started any level of verbalization at the age of five years.

Parties don't have to just have 'Happy Birthday to You' as their song – singing can be enjoyable for younger or less-developed ASD children. It allows non-verbal kids with ASDs to participate, even if they can only hum or approximate the words to a song. This is a social experience that can encourage interaction and help develop verbalization through mimicking and repetition. My son, for example, was able to sing many words that he felt unable to say – his repertoire of sung words eventually fed his ability to verbalize. ASD kids like the predictability of regular rhythms and choruses, which singing provides.

However, you must be prepared to either lead the singing or pay an entertainer to do so – don't expect these children to initiate the activity. Even if you are following recorded music, you or another adult will have to guide the singing. Singing games can involve simple childhood action songs such as 'Row, Row your Boat' or 'Heads, Shoulders, Knees and Toes'. These can become more enjoyable if you gradually speed up the tempo. Getting the kids to march around a room or garden can give ASD kids a sense of being part of a social group without expecting them to verbalize and they can engage socially in a limited and structured way.

Music games

Games which depend on music can work well, for example, 'musical bumps', in which the children sit down quickly when the music stops and the last one to do so is out (with a prize). It is easy to learn, involves the physicality that many ASD kids crave and is helpful for lower functioning ASD children. For higher functioning or Asperger children, try 'musical statues' in which they must stand perfectly still when the music stops and the one who cannot is declared out (with a prize). 'Musical chairs' can work – but using bean bags reduces any likelihood of injury, which some ASD kids might not understand as simply being a consequence of a physical game. After all, you don't want a party game to end up with tears or a meltdown!

'Corners' uses a simple idea of allocating a feature to each corner of a room or garden. This may be a colour or children's character, for instance. If you really want to be educational you can use facial expressions. You place a clear picture and name for each feature in each corner, then the children dance, walk, run or otherwise move to the music. When the music stops each child must run into a corner – whichever one they choose. Depending on the age and level of autism, you may well find the same children migrating to the same corner every time. Someone pulls out of the hat the name of one of the corners and everyone in that corner is out – with a small prize. This continues until one person is left.

Traditional games

As a principle, have a visual clue as to what the game entails and what the child is expected to do when participating. You may need adults to demonstrate and accept that several of the kids may not join in immediately, so factor this in, when timetabling.

Visual games such as 'follow the leader' can be easily accessed by ASD kids – they involve watching and movement, the first of which is a strength in most ASD kids and the second helps many such children de-stress. They also learn to take turns: 'Whose turn to be leader?' 'It's Chessy's turn to be leader' can be a mantra which encourages verbalization in lower functioning ASD kids.

'Colour copy me'

Following each other and using colours to indicate different actions develops good memory in many ASD kids. For example:

Saying RED = stop
Saying GREEN = run
Saying BLUE = star jump
Saying PINK = crouch down.

You can have a large poster with a key of what each colour represents and corresponding signs to be held up. An adult starts by demonstrating, then the children take turns to alternate whichever colour and subsequent action they want. This gives ASD kids the desired goal of being 'in charge' while experiencing fun, interacting with others.

'Simon says' is another useful traditional game. Remember to give a little reward to all children for participating. You can engage ASD kids by asking them to use their 'party companion' (their special toy for parties) to say the instructions instead of Simon. This gives ASD kids the element of control they enjoy, indulges their special interest in an educational way and encourages verbalization. For less able groups of ASD children, have a card showing instructions that the child 'in charge' can hold up to accompany instructions.

Games which involve little verbalizing enable ASD children with fewer verbal communication skills to still be social and involved in a party. These include 'hide and seek' and 'tag', both of which are easy to learn and demonstrate.

Use visual aids – such as a card to indicate whose turn it is – or play games that include chanting or a key word, such as calling 'Tag!' when a child tags another; this will develop communication in your ASD child and the guests.

SKILLS DEVELOPED

- verbalization
- turn-taking

- proprioception
- hand–eye co-ordination
- listening skills, following instructions.

'Duck, duck, goose'

All the children (and adults, if this supports the game) sit in a circle.

One person is the 'goose' and runs around the outside of the circle, gently tapping the others on their shoulders, saying 'duck' for each person until they choose a 'goose' at which point they say that word and start running.

The goose must get up and chase the other child, who has to run around the circle and try to get back to the new goose's spot in the circle before him.

Whoever gets to the spot on the circle last is the goose.

It sounds simple and it is! Its purpose for ASD kids is to engender a level of joining in with other children, of fun in a social event without necessarily the pressure to be competitive.

Games to try

What's in the box?

This game has to be micro-managed to ensure it works well. Get an adult to demonstrate the game first.

Place an object, hidden from view, in a covered box, which has two holes cut in the front. This object should be specific to an ASD child's special interest (gained from parents/caregivers prior to the party). The child should already be primed so that they are aware that the object is not scary but is something related to their current obsession.

The child inserts his hands into the two holes and feels the object. Encourage him to describe the object if he has verbal skills or just name it (approximately) if he has limited verbal abilities.

Don't prolong the experience – the lack of knowledge of what they might be touching can frighten some ASD kids.

The reward for participating is the object itself.

Get more confident ASD kids to participate first.

SKILLS DEVELOPED

- tactile sensory processing
- turn-taking
- manual dexterity
- imagination
- verbalization.

This can be a useful game if you are including a variety of activities in your party and the numbers of children invited are low – it is a rather adult-intensive activity.

Obstacle courses

We're not talking the armed forces here! An obstacle course is whatever you feel your ASD kids at the party can manage. This can be anything from crawling under a net and balancing on a beam to simply putting on and taking off a hat and gloves before moving on to the next 'obstacle'.

Other 'obstacles' for older, or higher functioning or Asperger syndrome kids might be:

- skipping a distance using a rope to the next obstacle
- swinging on a rope from one point to another
- climbing over an object to get to the next obstacle
- jumping from one obstacle to the next
- kicking a soccer ball from one point to the next
- throwing a ball or small bean bag into a receptacle from a distance.

Other 'obstacles' for very young or lower functioning ASD kids might be:

- saying or shouting a word or phrase (an approximation is OK)
- walking or running a very short distance
- jumping up and down on the spot several times
- crawling through a play tunnel
- showing a 'smiley' face
- moving a small pile of cards one at a time from one spot to another (make sure they don't feature a special interest of the child or those cards won't move anywhere!)
- throwing a bean bag
- catching a bean bag in a bucket
- drawing a shape on a large piece of paper.

The priority has to be on safety, so follow all manufacturers' guidelines on toys or games equipment.

You need sufficient responsible people to support each child along the course – for younger or lower functioning ASD kids this may be their parents/caregivers.

The children do not need to be competitively racing against each other – the objective is that each child reaches the end of the course in whatever time it takes them.

Reward all children for participating.

SKILLS DEVELOPED

- physicality and balance
- hand–eye co-ordination
- understanding of cause and effect
- verbalizing
- fine hand movement
- proprioception.

'Who/what am I?'

This tends to be a game for higher functioning ASD kids or those with Asperger syndrome but it could be adapted to other ASD children.

You put a picture and explanation or name of what the picture is, on a card and pin it to a child's back. Other children have to try and explain what they can see on the picture and the child with the card on their back has to guess what is on the card.

You can use ideas such as film characters, film titles or animals.

SKILLS DEVELOPED

- descriptive skills – describing, often in a detailed way, an object, person or place
- verbalization
- social skills – in a non-threatening way because physical contact is limited
- imagination
- listening skills.

'Snap' or 'Match'

Many ASD kids understand and can match objects which look alike. This can be extended to games in which lower functioning ASD kids can match shapes, or facial expressions, having chosen one – they then run around the room looking for a matching shape which another child will be holding. Both children can then be encouraged to say a given word or phrase, such as 'snap', 'match' or 'we did it!' This works well with large numbers of children or lower functioning ASD kids.

SKILLS DEVELOPED

- social skills – at a non-threatening level, involving little physical closeness
- visual memory
- physicality.

'Flip the kipper'

This is a team game, but each member takes it in turns to perform the task, working in a relay. Cut out one large fish-shaped piece of flimsy paper per team. Give each team a roll of newspaper, sticky-taped to stop it unravelling. When it's their turn each child has to use the newspaper to create a breeze to blow the 'kipper' to the next member of their team, who then blows the kipper to the next member and so on.

Everyone gets a prize for participating – and something slightly more for the winning team.

SKILLS DEVELOPED

- proprioception
- hand–eye co-ordination
- turn-taking
- spatial awareness.

Films

These are a good back-up to any party, so have a few available. Remember that chronological age is based on the development of typical children, so you may need a film designated for younger children than the ages of the ASD kids at your party. This do not need to be the latest blockbuster – repetition is a joy and comfort to ASD kids, so they may be very happy to watch a relatively old film. Do remember this is a back-up – ASD kids are renowned for their fascination with 'screen' activities (computers, TV, small screen games) so a film can dominate the whole party if you give it as an option.

Top tips

- Know the capabilities of the ASD kids you invite by liaising with parents/caregivers.

- Devise activities according to those capabilities, not the abilities of your own ASD child.

- Enlist plenty of help – whether this is parents/caregivers or other responsible helpers.

- Ensure the party plan and any rules of behaviours have various means of communication – pictures, words and clocks and times.

- Always have a quiet area (preferably a room) in case of emotional overload (meltdown).

- If things go wrong, remember that celebration parties are a challenge to all ASD kids – by holding the event and inviting other ASD children, you are broadening their ability to manage social situations in future.

- Feedback to parents/caregivers – both the positive and any challenging aspects of their child's time at the party.

TIPS FOR INVITING A CHILD WITH ASD TO A CONVENTIONAL PARTY

★ Communicate with parents/caregivers to discover the ASD kid's abilities and any issues – especially those that are known to cause emotional overload (a meltdown).

★ Try to accommodate those abilities and disabilities in the party activities – there is little point inviting an ASD child who is pathologically scared of water to a swimming party. However, if you have a variety of activities, the ASD kid has a greater likelihood of managing the event.

★ Remember that ASD kids often do not follow the typical pattern of development – so games for their chronological age may be well beyond their abilities.

★ Use a visual plan to show what's going to happen at the party – and make sure it happens! You may not want to be as strict as hosts of parties solely for autistic children, who give a rigid plan of activities and times. However, it will enable an ASD kid if you give a list of planned games or events – this gives the ASD kid much-needed predictability.

★ Make sure you allocate a responsible person to work one to one with the ASD child if the parent/caregiver cannot be there or wants a break.

Party Activities for 9–12-Year-olds

This chapter describes the particular issues for children with ASDs aged 9–12 years. For typical kids – and for some more developed kids with ASDs – this is a time when they attend celebrations for friends without their parents/caregivers. In itself this may create challenges for you as the host. It means that communicating with ASD kids' parents/caregivers is essential.

You may find that many of the games from the previous chapter are just as appropriate for ASD kids of this chronological age group.

The purpose of the chapter is to equip you with ideas for entertaining ASD kids in this age group during your party. All age ranges accommodate typical children. The actual experience of ASD kids will vary, since their behaviours and understanding will be moulded by personality, where they are on the spectrum, age and underlying conditions.

General features of ASD kids aged 9–12 years

Often, the older ASD children become, the wider the gap in development and maturity between them and typical kids. For children at the lower functioning end of the autism spectrum, receptive and expressive language may still be difficult – this is their ability to process language input from others as well as verbalizing. Additionally, these kids may continue to be overwhelmed by sensory stimuli and have poor emotional or physical development. All these factors contribute to the challenges of hosting any celebration.

ASD kids at the higher functioning end of the autism spectrum and those with Asperger syndrome, tend to have more subtle difficulties to manage. These issues may become more obvious as they reach this transition period between young childhood and being a teenager. During this time, ASD kids' lack of understanding of the nuances of verbal and body language becomes clearer; their literal interpretation of the spoken word and difficulty engaging in conversation are more patent. They develop a fuller understanding of their difference and start to gain insight into their position on the fringes of social communication.

Typical children of this age will be accustomed to the idea of winners and losers in competitive games and activities – don't assume this for their ASD counterparts. A recent party I attended with my nine-year-old autistic son was reduced to a tsunami of tears when one child was proclaimed the 'winner' and given the only prize for the activity!

Structuring the party

Structure is critical to any party with ASD kids – it enhances their understanding and reduces anxieties because they know what to expect. Predictability is extremely important to children on the autism spectrum.

In the absence of parents/caregivers, it is arguably more important to have clear rules for ASD kids. These should be sent home prior to the party, so that parents/caregivers can explain and work through them with their ASD child if necessary. Rules of the party should include:

- Acceptable and unacceptable behaviours – keep them simple. For example, 'No hitting' illustrated by a simple 'pinhead man' hitting another pinhead man, the latter crying and looking sad.

- Any sanctions if the children do unacceptable behaviours. It is often a good idea to make these a matter of sitting and watching the activity for a given time. Use a timer – an egg timer with grains of sand is highly visual and useful for ASD kids. Removing the child completely, especially if this is into a quiet room, full of sensory equipment, may in fact make the sanction more of a sanctuary – and you may never persuade the child to return to the party! You may link sanctions to the 'three strikes and you're out' or 'red card' rules of sports games – identify this in your rules, if so.

- That there are some out-of-bounds areas – show this with a sign and the wording that will be used (e.g. a hand, the words 'off limits!' all circled in red).

Remember that most autistic children are not rule-breakers and rule-benders – their lack of social understanding, literal use of language or lack of verbal linguistic skills are often what prevent them from complying with rules.

Some suggestions for typical children may fall flat with ASD kids. For example, crafts that involve fiddly pieces to construct jewellery or building objects can induce despair from ASD children who may not be dextrous, may not enjoy the experience of touching glue or different textures or may be so focused on perfecting their work that they become frustrated or unable to move on to the next activity.

You do not need to have many games – only two to four activities will be enough, especially if you have to explain to ASD kids and enable them to participate.

Activities for higher functioning kids with ASD/Asperger syndrome

Typical kids are ripe for team sports at this age. These older ASD children may be able to engage in team sports and often like the rules of competitive sports – but not necessarily. Playing as a team is contrary to the very being of many autistic kids. Additionally, such sports require physical contact which many autistic people find extremely uncomfortable.

Sports activities such as obstacle courses and 'solo' sports like swimming and trampolining are usually good choices – depending on information from parents/caregivers.

The skills sports can develop are:

- proprioception
- hand–eye co-ordination
- turn-taking
- balance
- social interaction from being in a team.

Skating

Beware ASD children who are preoccupied with skating boots – too tight, too loose, and too hard – which can dominate an entire party, reducing their experience to one of sitting at the side of the rink, adjusting boots continuously. Unless you have experienced and skilled responsible adults to help, you may struggle to get ASD kids on the ice and skating at all.

Skiing

You're looking at higher functioning ASD kids or those with Asperger syndrome if you're thinking of skiing. The level of co-ordination, spatial awareness and ability to focus, understand and follow safety guidance would exclude lower functioning ASD children. You also need sufficient responsible, skilled adults to enable your ASD kids. This may be no problem in countries where skiing is commonplace due to the climate – Canada, for example – but may be more of a challenge in places such as the UK where dry ski slopes are likely to be used and the possibilities of enlisting skilled helpers may be limited. It is a solo sport, so more comfortable for someone with ASDs.

Rock wall climbing

For safety reasons, this again will probably be an activity for higher functioning ASD/Asperger syndrome kids. This activity requires a high level of focused effort, planning of co-ordinated movements and physicality. For the correct ASD children/teens, this can be thrilling and absorbing. It feels relatively solo so appeals to many ASD kids on that basis.

Zip wires

Similarly, the safety elements attached to this sport ensure that it is more appropriate for higher functioning ASD/Asperger kids. Being a solo activity, it appeals to many such children/ teens.

Soccer, tennis, baseball and other team sports

The level of co-ordinated gross motor skills and understanding of rules, even the comprehension of winning and losing, are all more suited to higher functioning ASD kids or those with Asperger syndrome. The challenge will be enabling them to work as part of a team – but this will also be a crucial developmental experience. Do check with parents/caregivers about the likely success of any team sport, especially if it is the total focus of the party.

Ten pin bowling

Although they will be in teams, many ASD kids don't understand or enjoy the concept of team work and competition – this depends on their level of social and linguistic development. However, the fast-moving nature of ten pin bowling may give them a sense that their turn is coming and some may appreciate the idea of winning or losing against another team.

Music and dancing

I am not necessarily suggesting discos, where lighting and strobe effects could potentially induce extreme emotional responses or epileptic seizures. However, dancing in a non-competitive environment, with someone (an older typical sibling, perhaps) demonstrating how to look cool dancing, can be a winner for some girls (and boys) on the autism spectrum.

Discos need to be structured or they risk raising anxiety levels. Most ASD kids don't understand the joy in chatting to others and dancing freely. They crave a fixed timetable of how the disco will unfold. So have a period of dances where every one follows a lead dancer, either a person or on a televized game. Electronic games which show dance steps to follow and comment on your performance can be enjoyable and focus the attention on the TV rather than the individual child. Discos can be particularly difficult if mixed with typical kids, who derive pleasure and a sense of maturity from the unstructured environment that discos usually entail.

Singing karaoke, especially if they can watch themselves on TV, can be a winner.

Noise may be the challenge – so check with parents/caregivers before going down this route for your party.

SKILLS DEVELOPED

- verbalization
- motor co-ordination
- turn-taking
- listening and following instructions
- co-ordination of visual and motor function.

Creating from scrap

Building castles or cars or other objects of interest from craft materials can be good fun for kids with ASDs. The actual 'bricks' can vary according to the skills and development of the children involved. One piece of research (Owens *et al.* 2008) found that creating projects from Lego bricks and allocating children roles, which were rotated – such as the boss, the tool-finder and the maker – showed significant improvement in social skills and turn-taking.

There is no reason why this concept of allocating and rotating 'jobs' can't be used at parties, whether using Lego, other building blocks or scrap materials. The key is to ensure each child has a turn at each role. Due to the level of linguistic and social understanding this entails, it is suited to higher functioning ASD kids or those with Asperger syndrome.

My son had a party in which every child was given 'scrap' with which to create anything they wanted. These kids transformed old cardboard tubs, plastic tubes, bits of fabric plus lots of water-based glue and sticky tape, into dinosaurs, favourite TV characters and even a Tardis! Each child focused on their own fascination and they were completely occupied as a result. A theme would be difficult – because you'd lose ASD kids whose special subject was not your theme.

SKILLS DEVELOPED

- turn-taking
- imagination

- tactile desensitization
- fine motor movements.

Board games

These come in such a range that they accommodate a range of abilities on the autism spectrum, from your Asperger child who wants to play endless chess to the less able children who are hooked on sliding their way down snakes. Board games are predictable and bound by rules – both of which suit ASD children. They encourage taking turns and can be positive experiences as long as losing is seen as a logical consequence, not a disaster.

Card games

Card games often appeal to ASD kids because they involve following clear rules, memory and logic, all of which usually are strengths in ASD. In addition, social interaction and verbalization are limited in these games.

Imagination games

Forfeits

Forfeits tend to be more appropriate for higher functioning and Asperger children, who have a developed imagination which they can access. Forfeits can be simple, such as 'howl like a werewolf', at your Halloween party. They can be used if the child is the one who is 'out' in musical statues, for example.

Forfeits do not involve physical contact but do create social interaction, so can be constructive for ASD kids.

Charades

Charades are similarly more of a game for higher functioning and Asperger children. Many ASD kids avidly watch television and movies, so charades that use this knowledge can be useful.

They are more complicated and children will need support from responsible adults or older non-ASD kids.

You can explain the rules of charades using a visual poster, or have an adult demonstrate how to sign a movie, television show, etc. Working with an adult in this way is rudimentary team work and less threatening for ASD kids than teaming up with a peer. In addition, social interaction is encouraged without a need for extensive verbalization.

Mini obstacle course

If you want an indoor pursuit, try setting up an obstacle course using fine motor skills. For example, have each child suck on a large straw to lift peas from one container into another, or blow ping pong balls along a table, or use tweezers to pick up uncooked pasta and place them into a pot. At the end you could get each child to 'dunk' for apples (without the water) from a bowl – and eat the apple as a reward.

SKILLS DEVELOPED

- fine motor functions
- visual acuity
- oral functioning.

Activities and games for all abilities

Memory games

These can form part of a series of games and draw directly on an asset that many ASD kids have – good memory. For mixed ability groups or lower functioning ASD children, ensure that all written words are reinforced with pictures.

Pairs

Using large cards, such as flash cards of specific objects, lay them face down on the floor. Each child takes it in turns to turn over two cards, trying to get a match. If there is no match, the two cards are turned face down again.

This process can be started by adults who know to turn over different cards each time, while the watching kids will see which card is where.

Then the children take over. If they find a match, they take the next turn until they no longer find a match. The child with most matched cards is the winner – remembering to give all participants a 'prize'.

SKILLS DEVELOPED

- following visual cues
- visual processing
- turn-taking.

Fun games

Paint balling

Although avid paintballers might argue that it is skilled and highly competitive, this sport doesn't have to be! Unless they are physically disabled, children across the age groups and levels of ASD abilities can enjoy this game, which requires no physical contact with others and lots of physicality. The problems may stem from noise or disliking the feeling of being paintballed, which might reduce an ASD kid to great fear.

This is when discussions with parents/caregivers and clear explanations with the invitations are crucial to your party's success.

SKILLS DEVELOPED

- hand–eye co-ordination
- proprioception
- fine motor functions.

Balloon targets

Put a large target in the centre of the room on the floor. Give each child a balloon and help them blow up each balloon, but hold the seal, rather than secure it with a knot (some ASD kids may need considerable support doing this).

After a count of three, get the children to let go of their balloons and see which one gets closest to the target.

This game does not rely on specific skills which many of our ASD kids do not have, but on luck. It's also good fun and can make sounds that children will laugh at. This game can take a long time – purely because kids love it for its simplicity and funny aspects.

SKILLS DEVELOPED

- hand–eye co-ordination
- following auditory cues
- fine motor skills.

Baking

It is wise to use gluten and casein-free foodstuffs and make the exercise one of decorating cakes or biscuits or covering pizzas. With ASD kids who have a severely limited repertoire of foods they will eat, you may stumble with this activity because the 'prize' of course, is the food! This can act as one of a few activities during the party.

SKILLS DEVELOPED

- fine motor functions
- tactile input
- hand–eye co-ordination.

Although the above activities and games are not exhaustive, there are many in the previous chapter which may apply to this older age group. Remember that traditional games can be adapted to accommodate the needs of the ASD kids at you party or 'personalized' by using every child's 'party companion' toy as a participant in the activity. The key is to consult with parents/caregivers, especially if they are not accompanying their child to the party, and shape the party plan according to the abilities of your ASD guests.

Top tips

- Communicate clearly with parents/caregivers, who are less likely to be attending the celebration with their ASD child.

- Identify specific sensory or other issues for each ASD child.

- Ensure you have emergency contact numbers for parents/caregivers.

- Send out a plan of the party with the invitation, illustrated with pictures as well as key words.

- Make a list of acceptable and unacceptable behaviours which is posted on the wall and has pictures and words to illustrate meaning.

- Enlist plenty of helpers, especially as parents/caregivers may not attend.

- Allocate a responsible person to monitor each ASD kid.

- Always have a room where ASD kids can retreat if necessary.

- Give feedback to parents/caregivers – include positive as well as any challenging behaviours.

TIPS FOR INVITING A CHILD WITH
ASD TO A CONVENTIONAL PARTY

★ Remember that chronological age-appropriate games and activities may not be appropriate for ASD kids, whose development depends on where they are on the autism spectrum, any underlying medical conditions and age.

★ Communicate with parents/caregivers, asking their advice and giving them as much information as possible about the party plans and activities.

★ Allocate a responsible person to monitor the ASD child if the parents/caregivers cannot or do not want to attend or want a break in the course of the party.

★ Always have a quiet area – preferably a room – for the ASD child to retreat to, if necessary.

★ ASD kids may not understand body space and can cause typical children – particularly boys – to act aggressively when an ASD child stands too close. Educate typical kids before the party.

Parties for Teenagers

This chapter outlines the challenges for autistic teenagers, when their social skills and abilities to communicate are most highlighted. During their teen years, peers scrutinize each other's behaviours and appearance, which can lay bare differences between autistic and typical teens.

Celebration parties can emphasize difference still more and need to be handled sensitively.

The teen years, possibly, are the most sociable time in our lives – and therefore extremely challenging to ASD kids. The key objective of this chapter is to equip you with ideas for teen parties, which can educate and help ASD teens align themselves with acceptable behaviours and patterns of communication which diminish differences with their peers.

Typical teens

It is worthwhile considering typical teenage behaviours and challenges before focusing on the specifics of ASDs. The following are key features of teenage behaviour:

- Hygiene – either lack of attention to hygiene or over-indulgence.

- Organization – even kids who were highly organized as pre-teens can become the polar opposite! Responsible adults need to guide teenagers to develop good organizational skills. This can be a residual difficulty throughout life for kids with ASDs.

- Mood swings and general moodiness due to hormonal changes.

- Heightened hormone levels lead to desire for sexual relief and sexual partners.

- Masturbation is common in both males and females.

- Self-regulatory behaviours are not practised by most teens but are a crucial life skill to learn.

- Typical teens want to and will make their own decisions and mistakes.

- Teenagers often avoid any activities involving their family.

- Teenagers are often constantly hungry.

- Typical teenagers will communicate poorly with their family and challenge their parents, in order to develop a sense of independence and individuality.

- Non-compliance is almost a pre-requisite for being a teenager.

Adolescence and autism
Diagnosis

Although there is generally a greater awareness of autism spectrum disorders than there used to be, many children with Asperger syndrome are not diagnosed until the teen years – often resulting from contact with mental health services or the police. This is a particularly sensitive time for all youngsters and a time when most want to be like their peers, not different. A diagnosis of Asperger syndrome may earmark them as different to others and lower the individual's self-esteem at a critical point in their personal and social development. By contrast, parents/caregivers may feel quite differently, because they finally know why their child has specific quirks of behaviour and a history of social misunderstandings and few friendships.

Parents/caregivers

Many parents/caregivers become extremely anxious when their ASD children become adolescent because they think their children's autism has worsened. Occasionally, parents/caregivers report an improvement in behaviours and their ASD teen's ability to focus and learn in areas other than their special interest, due to hormonal and other changes during adolescence.

A useful experience is to have one teen on the autism spectrum and a teenage sibling who is not and acts as a yardstick for behaviours. For many parents/caregivers, though, they have more than one ASD teenager, which can be enormously challenging.

Perhaps the most frightening aspect for parents/caregivers is that they may feel they have little or no control over their ASD teenagers or the situations in which they become embroiled.

For many parents/caregivers, discussing sex and sexuality can be a hurdle with typical teenagers. These difficulties are heightened with ASD kids, who may have very limited communication skills, need visual images to understand concepts and explicit instructions about sexual behaviours.

ASD teens are often unaware of social cues and norms unless they are told in a direct and uncomplicated manner. Lower functioning ASD kids need to learn that they should lock bathroom doors when using the toilet – the temptation for parents/caregivers is to accompany their ASD child and not teach them how to manage toileting alone.

However, as the child matures and reaches puberty, they can be vulnerable to abuse and need to be equipped to understand privacy in bathrooms. Unlike typical teenagers, those with ASDs may not absorb knowledge of sexual norms from their peers or teachers. This information needs to come from parents/caregivers and should include inappropriate touch and requests to undress, and reporting back if these happen.

Responses to adolescence

ASD teens may struggle with physical changes and emotions that can overwhelm even typical teens. Depending on the level of communication skills they have, ASD teenagers may find explanations difficult to comprehend or confusing. Some ASD teenagers may be terrified of changes in the physical make-up of their bodies. They may fear waking up one day with all the alterations in their appearance having taken place overnight, because they cannot grasp the concept of gradual changes. Additionally, many ASD kids have high levels of anxiety, which they find difficult to manage. They may want to prevent their bodies looking different – growth of hair, larger breasts/hips – and may seek injurious ways to do this, for example, starving themselves of food or self-harming.

Inherent to ASD are challenges in empathizing and acknowledging or expressing feelings. Being a time of sweeping hormone levels and emotional turmoil, the teen years are particularly difficult for ASD kids.

Difficulties in communicating and mixing socially can cause ASD teens to be regarded as 'odd' or 'strange' just at a point in their development when, like typical teens, they are psychologically vulnerable. Higher functioning ASD teens and those with Asperger syndrome tend to have greater insight into feeling socially apart from their peers and this can directly lead to depression and self-harming behaviours, such as illicit drug or alcohol use.

Lack of social understanding can mean typical teenagers take advantage of ASD teens. In a similar way to typical teens, those with ASDs have problems resisting alcohol, tobacco and even illicit drugs. These may be more tempting to Asperger/ higher functioning ASD kids, who may be bullied by typical peers into substance misuse. Parties, if not monitored sufficiently, can become the source of drugs or alcohol.

Lower functioning ASD teens may lack the insight that they are different, because of the extent of their disabilities. They may need help with even basic daily activities.

Repetitive behaviours act as a comfort to ASD kids by being predictable and familiar and may become more pronounced in the teen years when so much is changing. However, stimming only serves to further alienate them from typical youths. Temple Grandin, a well-known, articulate speaker about autism, who has Asperger syndrome, describes how other teenagers used to call her the 'tape recorder' because she would verbally repeat what she had heard as part of her stimming behaviours (Grandin 1996).

ASD teens may become frustrated with their inability to date partners or create meaningful relationships. Coupled with an increasing sexuality, teenagers with ASDs can become hostile and angry with their lives.

If they possess insight, ASD teenagers may recognize that some ordinary rites of passage may not be open to them or may be fraught with difficulties. These include planning careers, finding employment, driving, getting married and having children. Again, the likelihood of depression is greater in these adolescents as they anticipate chronic hurdles in their future.

Teenage years are crucial to the individual developing a sense of self-esteem and exploring who they are. For ASD teens, who have an inability to comprehend the behaviours and language of their peers, it is a period when their self-esteem may be eroded or simply not grow. Clinical depression is relatively common in higher functioning ASD kids and those with Asperger syndrome (Ghaziuddin and Greden 1998) and militates against the development of a strong sense of self-worth.

The stress of expectations and responses of peers can make ASD teens anxious and even aggressive with their parents/ caregivers.

Puberty and sexuality

One key area of concern for many parents/caregivers is masturbation. In ASD kids this behaviour may be more extreme for the following reasons:

- They may not have the social awareness to know that masturbation should be a private activity, done in a private space, such as the child's bedroom or a bathroom with the door locked.

- They chronically use repetitive activities to provide themselves with comfort and reduce anxiety – masturbation serves this function.

- They may have fewer outlets for sexual relief due to difficulties establishing relationships.

You hope that parents/caregivers of the ASD kids you invite to your party will have talked with their teen about the boundaries around this behaviour – you may be surprised! I know of one case when the ASD teenager started to masturbate in the sitting room at home; the family abandoned the room to allow him 'private time'. This young man had not been taught that the sitting room was a public space and not an appropriate place for masturbating. If a similar child comes to your party, you could be in trouble!

You are unlikely to discuss masturbation with parents/caregivers prior to the party, unless they bring up the subject, so be prepared. If a child starts to self-stimulate at your party, I suggest you:

1   interrupt – don't hesitate or allow masturbation to continue

2   remind the child that there is a time and place for this activity – but a public area at social occasion is not it; be firm, but kind

3   distract the child by giving them another activity which is physical or requires concentration, or

4   distract the child by giving them something to engage in that requires both hands, or

5   direct the child to an appropriate private space, such as a bathroom – and ensure they lock the door

6   if ASD kids engage in frottage (rubbing genital areas against another person) you should tell them 'No' – and explain that this is not done in public.

Seizures

High hormone levels associated with puberty can cause seizures, even in those ASD kids who have never experienced them before. Around a quarter of lower functioning children with ASDs will have seizures as they reach adolescence (Edelson 2011). Seizures can be limited to absences, which last about ten seconds and are characterized by the child staring blankly, and then returning to task without realizing they have lost consciousness. Other ASD teens may have full-body, generalized seizures, when the child's entire body shakes violently, the face turns blue, the mouth can froth and the child drops to the ground – this requires urgent medical care.

Feedback any unusual behaviours to parents/caregivers, including aggression, which can indicate the onset of seizures (Edelson 2011).

Difference

Realization that they are different can be beneficial; some higher functioning or Asperger teens may work and learn better social skills to be 'cool' and fit in with their peers. For others, they may withdraw from social events and become more isolated – whether or not they feel a sense of loneliness is an individual matter; some people with ASDs prefer being alone to the constant challenges of society. Some ASD teens will migrate towards adult company because it feels safer and less challenging than trying to socialize with typical teenagers.

Structuring parties for higher functioning/Asperger teenagers

These ASD teens may attend schools or colleges alongside typical teens. This can produce social pressures as discussed above and a greater likelihood that your ASD teenager will want parties to include their typical peers.

Principles

Try to picture the worst possible scenario and work from that point. The most likely problems you will encounter will be:

- over-indulgence in alcohol – resulting in illness, accidents, damage to property
- use of illicit drugs – resulting in illness, accidents, damage to property
- gatecrashers – whom your child may or may not know
- too many people
- complaints from neighbours
- the police being called.

All teenagers cast a critical eye over your behaviours. Although you may be used to the clinical, direct questioning of higher functioning ASD/Asperger kids, you may not have had key social behaviours queried before. Expect questions about your drinking, smoking or drug-taking habits, past and present. This may also happen at any party you host.

Teenagers – whether typical or those with ASDs – need boundaries or rules within which they feel secure. In what can be a bewildering stage in their lives, when they cannot contain emotion and are developing sexually, teens need the solidity of you as a psychological anchor.

Part of the process of maturing for typical teens is pushing against those boundaries and trying to bend rules – standing firm, using a dialogue and understanding, enables typical teenagers to develop into adulthood. However, ASD kids are likely to adhere to rules you lay down – they like clear black-and-white information. Difficulties are more likely when they mix with typical teens who may manipulate ASD teens for their own advantage.

Remember that many teens with ASDs access social networking sites – sometimes more than typical teens because communicating may be easier for ASD kids when there is no eye contact, no body language to interpret and no pressure to be spontaneous in communication. In many ways, social networking is a means of ASD kids gaining confidence socially by practising social skills in a non-threatening environment.

However, the need to 'fit in' may be the very undoing of all your party plans. We all know tales of parties being advertised on social networking sites, resulting in colossal numbers of 'guests' and resultant damage to property – your own ASD teen may follow the path of typical teens, or the party could be hijacked by typical teens with whom your child associates.

Strategies

Remember that ASD kids need structure, especially as teenagers. A shorter, tightly structured party gives ASD teens security and less likelihood of engaging in unwanted activities: drinking alcohol, smoking or taking drugs to fill time.

1 If you have older, typical children, one strategy may be to give them (and a few of their friends) the role of 'bouncers' to effectively remain in the party and monitor what is happening while you, as the responsible adults, are in a different part of the house. You can be called on if problems arise.

2 Another strategy is a half and half party in which you invite ASD kids plus some trusted typical teens. Of course, being 'typical' does not preclude difficulties – the idea is to create an environment in which the ASD

teens can practise social skills without being humiliated and the typical kids still have a social event to attend. Don't assume that all typical teens want an alcohol and smoking fuelled party – good food, music and dancing can be a great draw. You should remain on the premises and monitor from a distance.

3   The mentor party is slightly different in that your typical attendees are fully aware that they are expected to model 'good' behaviours to their allocated mentee. You can recruit mentors from local high schools and have them hang out with their mentee during the party, in return for a meal at the party, work experience and a reference. Preparation is needed to ensure typical kids understand ASD and why ASD teens experience difficulties socializing. Mentors can enable ASD teens to practise starting 'small talk', for example, or to gain insight into body language, without encountering sarcasm or being teased. Typical mentors can also teach ASD teens standard, immediate responses to challenges from typical teens, for example, saying 'Whatever'. ASD kids have to learn such replies by rote.

This may not seem like a party to you and me, but it gives ASD teens the opportunity to be around other teenagers in safe settings, learning social nuances, practising being cool with few consequences and a sense of being part of a group which they may not get at school or in other social situations. Research has shown that this practical approach enables ASD teens to function more ably in social situations, in terms of initiating conversations, eye contact and wanting to attend social events (National Autistic Society 2011b).

Key points

- Do not supply alcohol or tobacco.
- Hide any alcohol in your home.

- Do not drink alcohol at a teen's party.
- Hide any valuable objects.
- Work out a strategy to monitor the progress of the party.

Party rules

These should be clearly displayed and unequivocal. Remember that some ASD teens will be taking prescribed medication. You might include statements about:

- alcohol
- illicit drugs
- smoking
- private behaviours in public
- aggression and fighting
- sex.

Remember that even teenagers with ASDs need structure and predictability. A yawning stretch of disco dancing with everyone chatting is a nightmare to ASD kids. They want a timetable, identifying a dancing time, in which they follow a leader or do action disco dances, such as 'YMCA', followed by singing using televized games for a given period of time, followed by food.

Lower functioning ASD teens

I have discussed in previous chapters possible activities and games that may suit younger children and will also be appropriate for those on the lower end of the autism spectrum. Many of these apply to lower functioning ASD teens, whose gap in social development may have widened still further from typical peers.

Parents/caregivers tend to continue to attend with this group of ASD teens. If not, I would recommend allocating a responsible adult to monitor each child, as with younger ASD kids. It is particularly important that same gender adults care for each child because the following issues may arise:

- Aggression – see following chapter.

- Masturbation or frottage (rubbing genital zones against another person) in public.

- Menstruation – parents/caregivers should communicate this with you, but it may be unexpected. Keep a supply of sanitary pads in the bathroom and if the parent/caregiver is not present, have two responsible women help the ASD teen with any practical issues.

- Emotional lability, hormones affect this group, producing rapidly altering emotional states, so expect tears!

Types of parties for ASD teenagers

Depending on the age of the teenagers, you can use structured games and activities, such as sports or paintballing. All the factors discussed in previous chapters relating to sports apply to teenagers, for example, physical contact being an issue. Often, physical activities are popular and important for teens, especially those with ASDs who may have high hormone levels and a level of hyperactivity associated with ASDs.

Top tips

- Regardless of chronological age, it is important to communicate with parents/caregivers.

- Get emergency contact details from parents/caregivers.

- If you need to allocate a responsible adult to a teen, ensure they are the same gender or that there are plenty of same gender responsible adults who could help.

- Enlist support from older typical siblings and responsible adults.

- Create and adhere to firm boundaries and rules of behaviour.

- Feedback to parents/caregivers.

 TIPS FOR INVITING A CHILD WITH ASD TO A CONVENTIONAL PARTY

★ Communicate with parents/caregivers about possible challenges for your ASD guests.

★ Get emergency contact details from parents/caregivers.

★ Be aware that ASD teens feel their difference keenly and may be vulnerable to manipulation by typical kids.

★ Focus on hobbies – these can facilitate conversations or enable an ASD teenager to manage the challenges of a party by becoming the party photographer, which reduces the pressure to talk or socialize conventionally.

★ Consider educating your typical guests about some challenges for ASD teens prior to the party.

★ Consider enlisting one or two responsible, typical teens to mentor and support your ASD guests.

What to Do When Things Go Wrong

The purpose of this chapter is to outline how to manage behaviours and challenges that may arise, despite parties and celebrations being carefully planned.

Throughout this book, I have emphasized the importance of planning and consulting parents/caregivers to diminish the possibility of unexpected events and this certainly is the best strategy. However, life is such that, even with typical children and teens, things will go wrong periodically – this chapter's key objective is to enable you to minimize the impact of unexpected and challenging behaviours and resume the party. The aim is to equip you with strategies to cope with difficult behaviours and provide a secure and calm environment for your party.

Unwanted behaviours

These might include:

- physically harming others
- being verbally aggressive
- damaging property
- drinking alcohol to excess or at all – depending on the rules of the house

- taking illicit drugs
- having sexual intercourse at a celebration.

Poor behaviour is the same for ASD or typical kids. Many people would argue that ASD kids don't intentionally behave badly because they follow rules – whereas many typical children and teens perceive rules as being there to be broken or bent.

If ASD kids learn what is and is not acceptable behaviour they tend to stick to those expectations. By the same token, ASD kids can be easily led into bad behaviours by typical peers, who may capitalize on their lack of social insight and persuade them to take inappropriate or illegal actions.

All human behaviour has a purpose or provides some function. Stimming behaviours in ASD kids are not 'bad' and, in fact, may comfort and soothe. Repetitive behaviours, such as rocking, can prevent meltdowns by giving the ASD kid a predictable, familiar activity to focus on.

Stimming should only be prevented if it is likely to harm another – but can often be modified. My son, for example, holds cutlery in one hand – one spoon and two forks, representing a head, two arms and hands. When he started this fascination, he tried to use two steak knives and a spoon. Replacing the knives, of course, was a priority for the sake of safety – his resistance to the change was muted by the fact that I exchanged the knives with another object, similar in weight, colour and size. Then I hid all the knives!

ASD kids may behave better without their parents/ caregivers' presence.

Reasons for unwanted behaviours

- Stress, caused by what they perceive as an unpredictable and confusing world. This tends to be more pronounced in children whose verbal skills are poor.
- Craving for sensory input or too much sensory stimulation. Some ASD kids appear to bounce off walls,

bashing into objects and being destructive – these are the ones who crave sensory input, such as physical activity. Those who seek cover, hide their eyes, their faces, retreat into their own world or try to walk out of the party altogether, generally are over-stimulated.

- Kids with ASDs may become easily frustrated and may not recognize that others can help them. By trying to manage alone, children with ASDs may become extremely frustrated, leading to unpredictable behaviours.

- ASD kids – particularly teenagers – may be teased for being different or your party may emphasize their difference, causing them distress.

- They may be responding to aggressive behaviours by typical children or teens at the party. ASD kids may not have a sense of body space, which means they invade others' personal space, sometimes resulting in aggressive behaviours by boys in particular.

- This same lack of understanding of body space can make typical girls feel intimidated by ASD boys and respond angrily or mockingly.

- Teenage girls with ASDs may be unaware of their sexuality and body space, so their actions can be misinterpreted, leading to unwanted behaviours by typical boys, for example. This causes the girls to behave unpredictably.

Prevention

Aside from communicating with parents/caregivers, carefully planning parties and conveying information visually, there are the following points:

- Write the rules of the party and expected behaviours on a clearly displayed poster on the wall in the main party room. As well as written words, draw behaviours – for example, draw one stick man pushing another and put a large red cross and the word 'No' next to the drawing.

- Be aware of physical signs that an ASD child is under stress. For example, non-verbal children may sweat, breathe heavily, appear agitated or have a wide-eyed look. Others may pose as if about to fight, clenching their fists or gritting their teeth. Non-epileptic seizures are also related to absolute rage or over-stimulation in ASD kids – they will fixate their eyes and effectively become unrousable for a period of time in an effort to block extreme feelings or stimuli.

- Have a sign that ASD children and teens can use to demonstrate that they're becoming distressed. This can be simple, such as a 'thumbs down' signal. With higher functioning ASD or Asperger kids, you may use a less obtrusive sign, such as using a key word.

- Depending on the organization of your party, you may have mentors modelling behaviours that are acceptable. ASD kids do not learn social behaviours by osmosis – it is a process of observation and reinforcement. ASD kids need to understand what is appropriate – simply chastising them for 'bad' behaviours is not constructive. Children and teens with ASDs need direction as to what specific behaviours are OK.

Managing changes to your party

Despite all the best preparation and planning, sometimes things go wrong – the entertainer is ill or the swimming pool leaks. So you have to explain changes to children or teens who are pathologically averse to change.

- Only make changes if there is absolutely no choice or resolution to the problem – investigate this before informing your ASD guests.

- Try to minimize the alterations to the plan, which your ASD guests will have seen and discussed with their parents/caregivers.

- Consider reorganizing the celebration for another day – this will largely depend on your ASD child and how well or badly he will take this decision and also how much notice this gives to everyone.

- Be visual in your explanation of the changes.

- Always create a back-up plan in case the first party plan goes wrong.

- Remember that ASD kids find change hard to manage and often dislike new activities with a vengeance.

- If you have to suddenly change games or activities, halt proceedings and do a quick drawing, reinforced by words.

- Changes will be facilitated if any new activity is either a physical one – such as trampolining – or one that is highly structured and can be explained visually.

Managing unwanted behaviours

It is clearer for ASD kids if you visually depict expected behaviours. Drawings of unacceptable behaviour, such as pushing someone under the water and a large red cross over the picture can be more helpful than just the words 'Don't push'. Also identify in pictures and words any sanctions for unwanted behaviours.

'Time out' – when a child or teen is removed from a given activity – may have limited use as punishment. Quite often, ASD kids are more contented away from the noise and disturbing environment of the party, so the conventional function of time outs is redundant. However, they do allow a break for 'cooling down' so can be helpful. Use a visual timer, such as a container with grains of sand.

Use your quiet room for emotional outbursts. This room is a safe space for ASD kids to retreat to act out and calm down. Prevention is key, so this room is best used before a crisis, allowing children to restore a balance before reintroducing them to the party.

Incorporate gentle music and headphones, which may help the ASD child have a period of internalization when he can de-stress. Sometimes time on a computer can enable a child with ASDs to feel comfortable again – the problem may be persuading them to leave the comfort of using the computer to rejoin the party. Many ASD kids adore computer time, when there are no expectations on them, when they are fully in charge and have no need to interact with others – so be aware that using computers to avert an outburst or reduce stress has a downside.

ASD kids who are crashing around your party, or behaving in very physical ways, often need sensory input. In a quiet room setting, provide heavy blankets or rugs which children can wrap themselves in, giving them weight and helping them feel grounded and secure. Rolling on large exercise balls gives some ASD kids the feeling of being weighted.

Some children with ASDs respond to what is termed 'resistive sucking' which focuses their energies and de-stresses them (Endow 2010). This includes using straws to suck up thick drinks, especially thin or long straws. Lollipops and popsicles or hard toffees or candies have the same effect. Chewy foodstuffs, such as dried fruits and gummy candies or sweets also act as stress reducers in some ASD kids.

With some ASD children hugging them hard is also helpful – depending on advice from parents/caregivers – or making them into a 'sandwich' by gently squeezing them between two large cushions. Quiet rooms can have cushions for the ASD child to fall into or hit with their fists to relieve stress and frustration. Squeezing flexible balls in the hands can enable de-stressing. Sometimes movement can be helpful.

A trampoline is a good way of de-stressing for many ASD kids. Swings which allow a regular, linear movement can be very comforting to ASD kids and teenagers.

The key principle is prevention. Use advice from parents/caregivers about what helps their child. Put ASD kids in a safe environment and allow them space and time to act out or retreat *before* unwanted behaviours happen.

Aggression

Like other behaviours, aggression is a way of communicating, albeit seemingly inappropriate and frightening at the time. Aggression may fulfil several functions, such as:

- demonstrating fear or stress
- attracting attention in a scary situation – sometimes in the hope of getting a time out
- showing hypersensitivity to sensory stimuli, such as noise
- avoiding situations or activities the ASD child does not want to engage in
- intense fear of making mistakes in 'typical' activities or situations
- pushing away others when the ASD kid does not have the ability to articulate discomfort or change the situation – for example, if other children are physically too close
- identifying that an ASD child has difficulty with social norms, such as turn-taking
- demonstrating that the child with ASD feels physically unwell, but cannot express or locate the illness
- signalling that an ASD kid has underlying epilepsy – seizures can occur at any point and are more common in ASD kids

- in teenagers, aggression may indicate fluctuating hormone levels and physical development
- demonstrating another emotion that the ASD kid cannot identify or articulate, such as frustration at being teased or not attracting girls.

Feed back aggressive behaviours to parents/caregivers. Doing so in a constructive way will enhance their knowledge about the ASD child and help them work out their own strategies to enable the child to attend future celebration events.

Meltdowns

Meltdowns are extreme emotional outbursts, typically involving injury to others and destruction to property. During a meltdown, children/teens with ASDs lose control of their behaviours completely, flailing limbs, throwing items, kicking, screaming or running about. The process can last for anything up to an hour, causing exhaustion to both the children/teens and their parents/caregivers.

Meltdowns have the potential to bring your party to a standstill. There are several reasons why meltdowns seem unexpected and shocking in ASD kids:

- It can be hard to 'read' an ASD kid's irritation with what is happening, so you may not see warning signs.
- Typical kids and adults may not consider the situations an ASD kid experiences as potentially irritating, so you may not anticipate a problem.
- ASD kids often do not have the facial expressions you might associate with annoyance or anger.
- Children and teens with ASDs tend not to express feelings through their voices – their tones may remain 'flat'.

- Kids with ASDs frequently express grievances as part of their usual repertoire of speech, so 'genuine' distress is difficult to see.

- If children/teens with ASDs are teased, they may not respond immediately but well after the event.

Reasons for meltdowns

ASD kids have difficulty reading the possible scenarios that may occur as a result of their actions or projecting into the future, so they don't understand the consequences of their behaviours. In my experience, one of the best ways of reducing meltdowns is to video record one and replay it for the ASD kid when they are calm – they can then visualize their actions and consequences. Without doubt, all behaviours have functions and causes, sometimes overt, sometimes subliminal. The following are the main reasons for meltdowns:

- Being teased or bullied – their different behaviours may be more obvious in social situations such as parties when stress or multiple stimuli may cause them to laugh or cry inappropriately and abruptly. ASD kids lack the social skills to be assertive or report if they are bullied or teased, so may respond with anger.

- Little sense of social pressure not to act out on stress – ASD kids have a poor grasp of how their extreme behaviours can affect others; their emotional development is delayed, often severely.

- Frustration – perhaps for not fitting in socially; perhaps due to an inability to 'get it right' in activities.

Principles behind dealing with aggression and meltdowns

1   Your own behaviour will reduce stress levels, if you are quiet and calm. Be 'with' the child, so that you focus

attention but only intervene to keep the child, other children or property safe.

2. Remove the child or teenager with ASDs to a quiet area and don't attempt to discuss the issues immediately. Wait until the outburst has finished before trying to engage them.

3. Try basic techniques such as telling the child to count to ten and/or take deep breaths.

4. Ensure that distractions are minimized in order to get full attention and prevent you having to compete with distractions – use your allocated quiet room.

5. Limited connection with their own feelings and lack of empathy with the emotions of others mean that ASD kids often respond better to any feedback from an incident using pictures. For example, draw what happened, and draw what you want to happen (the child sitting in the quiet room, then rejoining the party).

6. Some ASD kids find it easier to engage in discussions about events if you use the third person. So instead of referring to 'you' and expecting the child to talk about 'I' (the first person) the process can be discussed as 'person 1' and 'person 2' which enables ASD kids to participate. Some practitioners recommend using role plays and dolls to help re-enact the situation. This is long-term work – not something you could be expected to adopt as a party host!

7. Limit spoken words – typical children may respond to verbalizing but a stressed and emotional ASD kid will have even greater difficulty than usual in listening or verbalizing.

8. Give clear and simple instructions and allow time for the child or teen to absorb the information. Draw pictures and discuss returning to the party – then do so.

9 Refer to your list of behaviours that are acceptable or not, and their possible consequences, if appropriate. Be consistent and remind the child of future consequences of the same unacceptable behaviours at the party.

Resuming the celebration party

The less dramatic and obvious the unpredictable behaviours the more easily the child or teen can be reintegrated into the party. If you can keep responses to such actions calm, the child may de-stress sooner and be enabled to rejoin the celebration.

Encourage the child with ASD to return to the party. Poor experiences can remain with an ASD kid, so they are unwilling to engage in social events in future, based on one unhappy or stressful experience. This will limit the child's future development.

Act on what the ASD child communicates to you so that they understand the purpose and function of communicating. If they have an issue with a particular aspect of the party, tell them what action you will take (remembering not to promise something you cannot fulfil) and then demonstrate that you have taken that action.

Give the child or teen a key phrase to say if they feel stressed – or give them an allocated adult to approach to prevent recurrence of the same issue that caused unwanted behaviours.

Top tips

- Prevention is always better than having to manage a problem.
- Follow the plans in this book to try and prepare your ASD children and guests for what to expect at the celebration.

- Plan what strategies to use and who will intervene when things go wrong.

- Have plenty of helpers, especially if the ASD kids' parents/caregivers are not present.

- Remember that having ASDs does not excuse extreme and dangerous behaviours – you have the right to call the police.

TIPS FOR INVITING A CHILD WITH ASD TO A CONVENTIONAL PARTY

★ Consult with parents/caregivers.

★ Put in place strategies to prevent meltdowns and additional stress that might contribute to unpredictable behaviours.

★ Ensure you have contact details for parents/caregivers.

★ Don't take unpredictable behaviours as a reflection of your party or you – generally they are caused by stress.

★ Remember ASD kids and teens can be drawn into bad behaviours (as defined above) because they follow others. Lay down clear rules and guidelines and they will follow these instead.

★ Feedback to parents/caregivers if any incident has happened involving their ASD child.

CHAPTER 12

Conclusions, Further Advice and Support

Conclusions

The key to including ASD children in celebrations is to plan every party, based on the abilities of the ASD kids according to parents/caregivers or possibly directly from the kid with an ASD. Remember to feedback to parents/caregivers as well.

Use invitations as visual aids and ensure parents/caregivers and the children are aware of rules, a timetable of activities and any signage you might use in advance of the party. Social stories and visual aids enable understanding and make the party a more predictable event and therefore less anxiety-raising.

Draw on a pool of volunteers from local high schools. Give them an incentive to help – a meal and a job reference, for example. If you are part of a local autism support group, the pool of helpers could facilitate at a series of parties, which is good work and life experience for high school kids. A local autism support group may have someone who could give basic training to volunteers, so the entire process is educational.

ASD kids and parents/caregivers have a right to be included in what are considered rites of passage for typical children and teens. This inclusion also enables ASD kids to expand their social experiences and skills if well managed. As is the case with typical children and teens, once a successful party has happened, ASD kids may become part of a circuit of parties. Good experiences breed good experiences – and that's when parties become fun!

Agencies for further advice and support
United Kingdom
The **National Autistic Society** (www.autism.org.uk) gives advice and information to those affected by ASDs and their families.

Autism Initiatives UK (www.autisminitiatives.org) provides support and advice to those affected by ASDs and their families.

Coeliac UK (www.coeliac.org.uk) is a nationwide society offering information on gluten-free diets and products. Helpline: 0845 305 2060.

United States
Autism Support Network (www.autismsupportnetwork. com) has an active support network across the US offering advice on common issues around ASDs and contact with other parents/caregivers.

US Autism and Asperger Association (www.usautism. org) gives advice, guidance and support to people affected by ASDs and their families.

Autism Society (www.autism-society.org) has useful testimony from people affected by ASDs and their families, plus innovative approaches to autism.

US Department of Health and Human Services (www. hhs.gov) is the official government website with the latest information about autism in the US.

The Celiac Disease Foundation (www.celiac.org) offers information, gluten-free diets and conferences across the US.

The Celiac Society (www.celiacsociety.com) gives information and support with online gluten-free products. It covers all the US.

The website **www.celiac.com** gives information, support and gluten-free products.

Australia

Autism Spectrum Australia: www.autismspectrum.org.au/ a2i1i1l445l487/welcome.htm.

Autism Association of Western Australia: Email autismwa@autism.org.au.

Autism South Australia: Email admin@autismsa.org.au.

The **Autism Awareness** website (www.autismawareness. com.au/information/resources/websites) provides links to websites covering services across Australia.

Canada

Autism Canada: Email info@autismcanada.org.

Autism Society Canada: www.autismsocietycanada.ca.

Canadian National Autism Foundation: Email info@ cnaf.net.

Diagnosis of Autism Spectrum Disorders

Autism spectrum disorders (ASDs) are a range of conditions, identified by the presence of the triad of impairments (see below). A similar range of conditions are also called pervasive developmental disorders (PDDs), a term used by the International Classification of Diseases (World Health Organization 1993) and the United States' Diagnostic and Statistical Manual (American Psychiatric Association 2000). These conditions are:

- autism disorder/classic autism/childhood autism/ typical autism

- Asperger syndrome

- Rett syndrome

- childhood disintegrative disorder (CDD)

- pervasive developmental disorder not otherwise specified (PDD-NOS), including atypical autism (where symptoms do not fit wholly into an autism disorder diagnosis).

ASDs are characterized by difficulties in the so-called triad of impairments (Wing and Gould 1979) which are:

1 Social interaction, such as:

- lack of eye contact/covering eyes persistently

- reluctance to be appropriately tactile (hugs/closeness to family)

- aloofness or indifference to others
- no spontaneous attempts to make social contact
- lack of empathy with others
- following their own 'agenda' of (often seemingly odd) activities.

2 Social communication, such as:

- delay in speech
- not responding to their name
- echoing words or phrases, often out of context (echolalia)
- difficulty interacting with others
- difficulty expressing wants or needs – may use gestures
- not understanding spoken words as a way of conveying information.

3 Social imagination, such as:

- concentration on tiny things, not the overall picture
- inappropriate attachment to objects
- prolonged repetitive behaviours believed to stimulate one or more senses (also known as 'stimming', an abbreviated term for 'self-stimulation') (Nind and Kellett 2002)
- spinning themselves or objects
- lining up objects
- insistence on (often elaborate) routines
- inability to play with toys with any imagination
- displaying tight, repetitive interests.

Asperger syndrome

A diagnosis of Asperger syndrome, as defined by the American Psychiatric Association and the World Health Organization, can only be given if the child has typical development of verbal language and other cognitive skills. In higher functioning autism, speech and/or cognitive functioning are delayed in childhood (American Psychiatric Association 2000; World Health Organization 1993).

The key signs are:

- difficulties with social communication – taking verbal language literally, missing the nuances of spoken or body language, unusual verbosity or misunderstandings, such as not taking turns in conversation

- obsessive and ritualistic behaviours – often accompanied by encyclopedic knowledge of self-chosen subjects

- poor co-ordination skills and sensory difficulties.

There is ongoing debate about Asperger syndrome; some believe it should not be included on the autism spectrum. Although others argue that Asperger syndrome is not discrete from autism disorder, Ver Ploeg (2009) asserts that some key elements are different:

- In autism disorder, there is an apparent global, emotional disconnectedness from the social world. She argues that although people with Asperger syndrome demonstrate specific difficulties with their perception of non-verbal communications and in drawing social inferences, they have a basic connection with the social world.

- In autism disorder, people lack the ability to empathize, whereas those with Asperger syndrome can show empathy.

- Children with Asperger syndrome can feel intense loneliness derived from feeling on the periphery of the social world. This is not an emotion associated with autism disorder.

Communication Methods

The Picture Exchange Communication System (PECS)

PECS was developed in 1985 as a means of supporting communication for people with autism spectrum disorders and other special educational needs. It involves using picture symbols which depict, for example, an object or action, always with the name of the object or action on the picture card. Anyone enabling communication using PECS undergoes a level of training to ensure they give appropriate prompts and responses to the student – two people work with the student initially to promote the basic theory of exchanging a picture for a desired object, reinforcing the request with spoken words.

Makaton

Makaton signing is a language programme based on a simplified form of British Sign Language. It incorporates signs (using hands) and symbols (usually on cards or in books) to enable people to communicate. Crucially, the spoken word is used in combination with signs and symbols, the purpose being to ultimately produce verbalization. Makaton is a flexible tool to promote speech.

Visual cues

These are any visual aids which enable understanding by people with ASDs. In schools, visual timetables are commonly used, showing times – and often a picture of a clock – of activities throughout the school day. Simple drawings of each activity enable children with ASDs to know what will happen next – a predictability that autistic children find comforting. Visual cues also include signage such as pictures on bathroom doors to depict whether these are girls' or boys' facilities, or a photo of the child and their name by their coat hook.

Another visual way of enhancing the understanding of those with ASDs is using comic strips, in which emotions, for example, can be colour coded or earmarked with symbols. Dissecting conversations enables people with ASDs to clinically gain the meaning of social interactions and learn (often by rote) how to respond to social situations.

Social stories

These were developed in 1991 by a teacher, Carol Gray, as a way to teach social skills to people on the autism spectrum (see www.thegraycenter.org). They are a series of pieces of information about social situations, new people and places. They can be used to demonstrate 'acceptable' and 'unacceptable' behaviours, for example, what to do if you are angry. People with ASDs have difficulty picturing themselves in potential social situations and little knowledge of what to expect of others and what will be expected of them – social stories enable them to examine possible scenarios without the pressure of the reality of the situation. People with ASDs can practise responses using the information in social stories.

Social stories are often about what seem mundane subjects to a typical person and examine the minutiae of social situations. They are usually short, which reflects the attention span of the autistic person who is learning from them.

Many people with ASDs still need pictures to facilitate their understanding as well as written words. The most effective social stories are tailored to the individual person with ASD and are written as a straightforward description. Pictures – like a cartoon strip – enhance understanding for those with ASDs.

References

Adams, J. and Holloway, B. (2004) 'Pilot study of a moderate dose multivitamin/mineral supplement for children with autistic spectrum disorder.' *Journal of Alternative and Complementary Medicine 10*, 6, 1033–1039.

American Psychiatric Association (2000) *Diagnostic and Statistical Manual of Mental Disorders* (4th edition, text revision) (DSM–IV–TR). Washington DC: American Psychiatric Association.

Baird, G., Simonoff, E., Pickles, A. *et al.* (2006) 'Prevalence of disorders of the autism spectrum in a population cohort of children in South Thames: the Special Needs and Autism Project (SNAP).' *The Lancet 368*, 9531, 210–215.

Centers for Disease Control and Prevention (2012) 'Prevalence of Autism Spectrum Disorders – Autism and Developmental Disabilities Monitoring Network, 14 Sites, United States, 2008.' *Center for Disease Control's Morbidity and Mortality Weekly Report*, March 30 2012. Atlanta: Centers for Disease Control and Prevention.

Coeliac UK (2012) 'Nutritional deficiencies and supplements.' Available at www.coeliac.org.uk/healthcare-professionals/diet-information/nutrional-deficiencies-and-supplements, accessed on 23 April 2012.

Edelson, S. (2011) 'Autism, Puberty and the Possibility of Seizures.' *Autism Research Institute.* Available at www.autism.com/ind_puberty_seizures.asp, accessed on 30 January 2012.

Ehlers, S. and Gillberg, C. (1993) 'The epidemiology of Asperger Syndrome: a total population study.' *The Journal of Childhood Psychology and Psychiatry 34*, 8, 1327–1350.

Elder, J.H., Shankar, M., Shuster, J., Theriaque, D., Burns, S. and Sherrill, L. (2006) 'The gluten-free, casein-free diet in autism: results of a preliminary double blind clinical trial.' *Journal of Autism Developmental Disorders 36*, 3, 413–20.

Endow, J. (2010) *Practical Solutions for Stabilizing Students with Classic Autism to be Ready to Learn – Getting to Go!* Kansas: APC Publishing.

Ghaziuddin, M. and Greden, J. (1998) 'Depression in children with autism/pervasive developmental disorders: a case-control family history study.' *Journal of Autism and Developmental Disorders 28*, 2, 111–115.

Golnik, A.E. and Ireland, M. (2009) 'Complementary alternative medicine for children with autism: a physician survey.' *Journal of Autism and Developmental Disorders 39*, 7, 996–1005.

Gould, J. and Ashton Smith, J. (2011) *The Diagnosis and Education of Girls and Women with Autism.* London: National Autistic Society.

Grandin, T. (1996) *Thinking in Pictures: And Other Reports from My Life with Autism.* London: Bloomsbury.

Jyonouchi, H. (2004) 'Adverse reactions to dietary proteins in children with autism.' *The University of Medicine and Dentistry of New Jersey Research* (Winter 2004). Available at www.umdnj.edu/home2web/research/publications/winter_04.pdf, accessed 30 January 2012.

Kanner, L. (1943) 'Autistic disturbances of affective contact.' *Nervous Child 2*, 217–250.

Kern, J.K., Miller, V.S., Cauller, P.L. *et al.* (2001) 'Effectiveness of N,N-dimethylglycine in autism and pervasive developmental disorder.' *Journal of Childhood Neurology 16*, 3,169–173.

Le Breton, M. (2001) *Diet Intervention and Autism: Implementing the Gluten Free and Casein Free Diet for Autistic Children and Adults – A Practical Guide for Parents.* London: Jessica Kingsley Publishers.

Lehrer, T. (1959) 'Bright College Days,' *An Evening Wasted with Tom Lehrer.* RCA Studios.

Marchetti, B., Scifo, R., Batticane, N. and Scapagnini, U. (1990) 'Immunological significance of opioid peptide dysfunction in infantile autism.' *Brain Dysfunction 3*, 5, 346–354.

National Autistic Society (2011a) 'Higher-functioning autism and Asperger syndrome: what's the difference?' London: NAS Publications. Available at www.autism.org.uk/about-autism/autism-and-asperger-syndrome-an-introduction/high-functioning-autism-and-asperger-syndrome-whats-the-difference.aspx, accessed on 30 January 2012.

National Autistic Society (2011b) 'Glasgow Mentoring Project.' London: NAS Publications. Available at http://www.autism.org.uk/get-involved/volunteer/glasgow-mentoring-scheme.aspx, accessed on 30 January 2012.

Nind, M. and Kellett, M. (2002) 'Responding to individuals with severe learning difficulties and stereotyped behaviour: challenges for an inclusive era.' *European Journal of Special Needs Education 17*, 3, 265–282.

Owens, G., Granader, Y., Humphrey, A. and Baron-Cohen, S. (2008) 'LEGO therapy and the social use of language programme: an evaluation of two social skills interventions for children with high functioning autism and Asperger Syndrome.' *Journal of Autism and Developmental Disorders 38*, 10, 1944–1957.

Reichelt, K.L. *et al.* (1981) 'Biologically active peptide-containing fractions in schizophrenia and childhood autism.' *Advances in Biochemical Psychopharmacology 28*, 627–643.

Rimland, B. (1964) 'Infantile autism: the syndrome and its implications for a neural theory of behaviour.' New York: Appleton-Century-Crofts.

Strickland, E. and McCloskey, S. (2009) *Eating for Autism: The 10-Step Plan to Help Treat your Child's Autism, Asperger's or ADHD.* Da Capo Press.

Ver Ploeg, A. (2009) 'Aspergers Kids and Social Skills: Home and School.' Website: My Aspergers Child: Help for Parents with Children who have Aspergers/High Functioning Autism. Available at www.myaspergerschild.com/2009/06/aspergers-kids-social-skills-home.html, accessed on 30 January 2012.

Whiteley, P., Shattock, P., Carr, K. *et al.* (2010) 'How could a gluten and casein-free diet ameliorate symptoms associated with autism spectrum conditions?' *Autism Insights 2*, 39–53.

Wing, L. (1981) 'Sex ratios in early childhood autism and related conditions.' *Psychiatry Research 5*, 2, 129–137.

Wing, L. and Gould, J. (1979) 'Severe impairments of social interaction and associated abnormalities in children: epidemiology and classification.' *Journal of Autism and Developmental Disorders 9*, 1, 11–29.

World Health Organization (1993) *The ICD-10 Classification of Mental and Behavioural Disorders: Diagnostic Criteria for Research.* Geneva: WHO.

Yale Child Study Center (2011) 'Autism.' Website: Autism Program at Yale. Available at http://childstudycenter.yale.edu/autism/information/autism.aspx, accessed 30 January 2012.

index

Parent Power

Because your family matters ...

Family Matters is a new series from Wiley highlighting topics that are important to the everyday lives of family members. Each book tackles a common problem or difficult situation, such as teenage troubles, new babies or problems in relationships, and provides easily understood advice from authoritative professionals. The *Family Matters* series is designed to provide expert advice to ordinary people struggling with everyday problems and bridges the gap between the professional and client. Each book also offers invaluable help to practitioners as extensions to the advice they can give in sessions, and helps trainees to understand the issues clients face.

Titles in the series: